JUMP START
YOUR
MORTGAGE
CAREER

JUMP START
YOUR
MORTGAGE
CAREER

AMEEN KAMADIA

Published by Kamrock Publishing LLC, Houston, Texas.

www.MortgageBrokerTraining.com

For information on multiple copy discounts, licensing, or affiliate programs, please contact the publisher at the website listed above.

More information on Ameen Kamadia's award winning newsletter and one-on-one counseling is also available at the website listed above.

This publication is designed to provide general information regarding the subject matter covered. However, laws and practices often vary from state to state and are subject to change. Because each factual situation is different, specific advice should be tailored to the particular circumstances. For this reason, the reader is advised to consult with his/her own advisor.

The author has taken reasonable precautions in the preparation of this book and believes the facts presented in the book are accurate as of the date it was written. However, neither the author nor the publisher assumes responsibility for any errors or omissions. The author and publisher specifically disclaim any liability resulting from the use or application of the information contained in this book, and the information is not intended to serve as legal advice.

ISBN: 978-0-9753756-3-1

Printed in the United States of America

Library of Congress Cataloging-in-Publication data available upon request from the publisher.

A FREE GIFT FOR YOU!

If you are truly serious about the mortgage profession, there is a FREE resource you must become familiar with. It is called Mortgage Magic.

This tool will teach you more than you ever dreamed of knowing regarding marketing, mortgages, borrowers, and everything related.

SOME OF THE THINGS YOU WILL LEARN ARE:

- How to increase your customers' credit scores.
- How to spend less money on marketing and get better results.
- How to have Realtors eating out of your hands.
- The proper method to follow up with leads and double your income.
- How to automate your marketing.
- What factors cause homebuyers to choose one lender over another. And it's not the price!
- How to make your prospects an offer they can't refuse.
- And a lot more.

All this is brought to you FREE from the publisher of this book. All you have to do is visit the following website:

http://www.MortgageMagic.info

DEDICATION

I dedicate this book to my mom,
for all your loving, caring and nurturing.

Thank you for everything.

I Love You.

TABLE OF CONTENTS

Introduction

"How do I become a successful loan officer?" That's a question we get asked a lot at MortgageBrokerTraining.com. And the answer is different for everyone. For the purposes of this book, we are going to focus on financial and business success. So the question becomes,

"How do I set up my business so that it generates a large number of loans, generates large commissions, and leaves me with enough time to do the things I enjoy?"

That is the question I attempt to answer in this book. But I cannot turn you into a success alone. You must be the main actor/actress in this drama. I can only be the director. As a team we can be unstoppable, but only if we work as a team, and start with the basics.

Becoming a success in the mortgage business is not hard. Several thousand people make a very good income at it every year. A handful make millions every year. On the other hand, there are those that come and go within a year. What is the difference? Why do some people succeed while others fail?

Man has been asking that question for centuries. And it is not my place to say that I have the answer. I don't. The reason is different for everyone. But there are ways to make sure that failure does not happen to you—if you are willing to succeed.

What does it take to succeed as a loan officer?

It takes hard work, it takes a bit of time, it takes knowledge, it takes gumption, and it takes sacrifice.

But you already knew that didn't you?

What we want to do in this book, is to provide the essentials, the basics, the knowledge of what to do to become successful. Make sure you read every chapter and truly understand the concepts. Then, you will be able to complete the 30 Days to Success Plan at the end of the book. If you try to jump to the back without understanding the concepts, you will not as successful as you could be.

There is a price to pay for success. If you pay up, being a loan officer can be the easiest, highest paid profession. If you avoid paying the price and try to jump the gun, you will find that you would be better off working "a real job".

IF YOU ARE NEW TO THE MORTGAGE BUSINESS

What you are about the learn, and the steps you will take in the 30 Days to Success Plan, will put you above 95% of loan officers in the market today. The Plan will probably take you longer than 30 days to finish. Most do not finish on time. It is time and labor intensive. And that is because I feel that you need to be up and running as soon as possible. Especially if you are like most and working on commission. You cannot afford to go 2–3 months without any income. We want you to be generating loans while you are learning. It's on the job training to the max.

The mortgage business can be tough, or it can be easy. The actions you take in the beginning of your career will dictate how well you do. Follow the plan, understand it, and pay the price now, so that you can reap the rewards later.

IF YOU ARE NOT NEW TO THE BUSINESS

If you are an experienced loan officer, you still need to go through all the material. There is a reason you picked up this book, and you shouldn't let your pride get in the way. If something is too basic, or you have already done it, read that section anyway. Even one great idea could turn around your business. Then use the other parts of the book to strengthen or change what you are doing now.

Remember, everything presented is backed by fact. Everything described works, and can work for you if you try. Do not casually brush a technique aside without testing it. Some of the ideas presented might go counter to what you have been told before. I don't care if you think a particular strategy will not work. I already know it does because I have used it and seen it done by countless others who are successful.

Before you go any further you need to realize a few things. If you are not where you want to be in your career,

- it is not because a certain strategy didn't work,
- it is not because the economy is bad, and

- it is not because all homebuyers just want the lowest rate.

There are no quick fixes; becoming a success takes time.

If you go through the book and pick and choose what you will do and what you won't, you are the only one who will suffer. I am not offering you a buffet where you take only that which you like best. You must do it all. And it is the items that you don't want to do that will help you the most.

You might even know about everything in here. But if you do not use the knowledge, it is the same as not knowing it at all. Make a commitment to yourself that you will follow through with everything laid out, and that you will not let your pride get in the way of success.

You can be the smartest, most educated, best looking, best dressed, most trained, most experienced loan officer in the world with 15 zillion loan programs and zero interest loans until infinity, but without clients you will still starve.

Loan officers deal with money. It is our job. It is what we do.

Loan officers can make a lot of money. We get paid on commission. And that is because our job, our primary purpose in this line of work, is to get loans.

Without loans a loan officer is nothing. Just taking up space.

With loans, a loan officer is on top of the world.

This book has been written to help you to the top of the world.

This book is for new loan officers just getting into the business and for experienced ones that are in a sales slump.

In it, we will cover the basics of mortgage marketing.

- How to market yourself, your company, and your product (in that order).
- How to program your mind to achieve success.
- How to skip the mortgage marketing learning curve.

Using this book as a primer, you will be able to move from zero loans to tangible income if you follow the instructions.

My first introduction to the mortgage business was a little different than yours. I had no book to teach me how to get loans, I had no website such as MortgageBrokerTraining.com to learn from. All I had was a license and some idea of how to fill out a 1003. No friends to ask for a loan. No family either. I was a mortgage loan officer that lived in an apartment.

But I made it. I started small. In the beginning, one loan a month was all I needed. But some months I didn't even get one. Then I started doing two, then more. Until I was able to open my own company and hire others.

So do not despair if times are tough. I have been there. Many of my now successful students have been there. If we can do it, you can do it.

All you need to do is approach this material with an open mind and try it. It works. It has worked in the past, and is working right now.

The ideas and strategies in this book will get you to think in new ways. Marketing is more than just running ads and waiting for the phone to ring.

Marketing is everything you do. There is a marketing component in every action your business takes. I have seen real estate agents with their magnetic signs on their car doors driving around cutting off other cars in traffic. For them, their poor driving is marketing—negative marketing.

The way you walk, talk, dress, sit, and stand all impact whether you will get the loan or not. The words you use are just as important as the rate you quote.

Let me let you in on a little secret: The lowest rate, doesn't always get the loan.

In fact, the loan officers that do the most business, and make the most money, usually charge the highest in fees. You will learn why and how in this book.

There are several key elements that you need to know to succeed as a loan officer. Many of them are in this book. Implementing these strategies will indeed give you a Jump Start.

If you need further help or would like to learn even more about marketing, we have developed an online class also called

Jump Start Your Mortgage Career. It continues where this book leaves off.

There is more than a few months worth of work in this book for you. But there is only so much I can fit into a book. The class is much more intensive (2 lectures a week for 11 weeks, reading assignments, and homework).

It is so intensive that we guarantee that you will have loans when you finish if you just do the homework assignments. If you want to take your business to an even further level, you can get more information about the class at our website, JumpStartYourMortgageCareer.com.

So after you are done here, check it out. And if you need any clarification or further explanation of any of the concepts in this book, shoot me an email, and my staff and I will reply as best we can.

Good Luck, and May All The Loans Be Yours,

Ameen Kamadia

SECTION 1
START WITH THE BIG PICTURE

Before we dive into generating leads and converting those leads into loans, we are going to do a little work on you.

If I were to ask you, "What do you sell?" what would your reply be?

Money?

Home Ownership?

Peace of Mind?

Nope. You only have one product to sell—you. If a prospect doesn't like you, he has a million other places he can go to get the exact same loan at the exact same price. The only difference between them and you, is you.

So that is where we are going to start.

The purpose of Section 1 is to get you thinking like a first class marketer. These first few chapters will introduce you to concepts that might be new to you, but are essential to your business.

As a loan officer, you work for yourself. You are your own business. It doesn't matter what company you work for. In most cases, if you do not produce, you do not eat, and soon you won't have a job either. Your #1 focus should be on your business. You are the CEO, President, Chairman of the Board, and Owner. You rule. But if you don't know what you are doing, there is not much hope for success.

If you are new to the business, consider yourself lucky. You are going to learn all these business building techniques before you start building your business. On the other hand, if you have been in the business for a few years, or already have a somewhat successful business, you will kick yourself once you realize how much more business you could have been doing all along.

Your business is like a skyscraper. One day soon, it will be towering above the earth. But right now, all you have is a plot of land and an idea. An idea that you are going to become a world-class loan officer, your business is going to help you achieve all your financial goals, and allow you to live life the way you were meant to live it.

The first step to build your skyscraper (business) is to design it. How can you just start building without knowing what it is going to look like? The next step is to pour the foundation. The higher you want your skyscraper, the stronger your foundation must be.

That is what we are going to do in this first section. Design your business, and pour a solid, strong foundation on which to start building. So let's get started.

HOW TO GET
WHATEVER YOU WANT

What is it you desire?

When was the last time you just sat around dreaming?

I envy young kids for a lot of reasons, and one of those is because they are great dreamers.

As adults, we get jaded. Things don't work out. We realize or are told "the ways things work" doesn't always fit in with our dreams. So the dreams die and we get stuck.

We don't move forward or get what we want because we stop dreaming.

But there is a powerful way to change that.

GOALS!

The process of setting and managing goals lets you have wherever you want personally and professionally.

Goals give you long-term vision and short-term motivation. They focus your learning efforts and help you organize resources.

Goals are all about purpose. With purpose, you can set goals and overcome obstacles. Without goals, life gets confusing and haphazard.

You can't get to the stars if you are aiming for the sea.

Many people know what they should do. Having great success is no big secret. Still, most people don't do what it takes to achieve that success.

It's not a matter of energy. It's a matter of goals. Tony Robbins' response to people who say they are lazy is, "You're not lazy. You just have impotent goals!"

By setting goals you can:

- Achieve more.

- Improve performance.

- Increase your motivation to achieve.

- Increase your pride and satisfaction in your achievements.

- Improve your self-confidence.

- Eliminate thoughts and attitudes that hold you back.

Goals add up to one big plus. Research has shown that people who set goals effectively suffer less from stress and anxiety, concentrate and perform better, and are happier and more satisfied.

WOW. That's some good stuff.

Success in the mortgage business, or any business, is much easier when you have proper goals.

You might be wondering why a book on marketing starts off with a chapter on goals. Simple. Unless you train your brain, you will not be able to achieve the level of success you deserve.

Marketing can help you get leads, but your goals can help you get up in the morning. They can help you go the extra mile with a customer, which can result in several referrals.

Goals motivate you. Your goals are the reason you work. They are the reasons you do what you do. Without them, without something to look forward to, without some reward, life becomes boring and stale.

EFFECTIVE GOAL SETTING

Goal setting is more than scribbling ideas on a piece of paper. Our goals need to be complete and focused, much like a road map. In order for something to be a goal:

- It has to be important to you personally.

- It has to be within your power to make it happen through your actions.

- It has to be something you have a reasonable chance of achieving.

- It must be clearly defined and have a specific plan of action.

You need to think about crafting goals, starting with the big picture of how you want your life and business to look.

FIRST THINGS FIRST

Prior to starting a goal-setting exercise, work through these steps.

Become a child again.

Go back to a time when anything was possible. Go back to your childhood—when your imagination had no limits. What did you want to be when you grew up? Maybe you were like me. I wanted to be six things at once: a writer, a super hero, a billionaire, an engineer, a famous celebrity, and an astronaut. Those were the days, weren't they? We weren't limited by responsibilities, time, or the laws of physics. We could just imagine.

That is what you need to do now. Anything is possible once again. You are about to learn the techniques to get as much money as you want. Whatever you can imagine, you can have.

Make a list of your values.
What's really important to you? Decide on your most crucial values, and make sure the goals you set are designed to enhance them.

Begin with the end in mind.
Create a clear image of what you want your business and your life to look like.

Project yourself into the future.
Envision your life five, ten years from now. What does your daily routine look like? Your family? Your bank account? Begin to think as though you are already experiencing the success you seek.

Ask yourself good questions.
As you think about your goals, ask yourself HOW you can make them come true. Your mind will respond to such a question more effectively than if you just make statements or wishes.

THE SIX AREAS OF YOUR LIFE

Take out a notebook and follow along as I walk you through these exercises. I won't take no for an answer. If you want to really Jump Start your business and life, it starts here, on this page. You can do everything else in this book, but if you do not do these simple exercises, you won't accomplish one-tenth of what you are capable of.

Ready? Here we go.

We are going to create goals for each of the six areas of your life:

1. Business/Financial

2. Personal Development/Social

3. Spiritual/Mental

4. Physical

5. Fun/Enjoyment

6. Contribution

Write the name of each area across the top of a separate piece of paper.

Take at least five minutes for each area and write down everything you want. Don't try to be specific. Write as fast as you can and get as many down as you can. Take more than five minutes if you must, but don't stop. We will get into specifics later.

In the Business/Financial area, write goals for your income, net worth, investments, business development, business growth, time spent working, retirement date, career, and anything else you can think of.

For Personal/Social goals, write about your relationships with your family, spouse, children, friends, and who you want to be as a person.

For Spiritual/Mental goals, write how you wish to interact with your Creator, what you want to learn, what skills you want to master, what books you want to read, etc.

For Physical goals, write how much you want to weigh, how often you exercise, what you eat, how long you can hold your breath, and any physical feats you want to accomplish like running a marathon or raising five kids.

For Fun/Enjoyment goals, write where you want to travel and what you want to buy: a new car, house, jewelry, a new wardrobe, a Lear Jet, a season ticket to your favorite NFL team, you name it.

For Contribution goals, write what kind of difference you are going to make in the world: adopt a child, start a foundation, raise money for charity, organize a food drive for the homeless, etc.

Defining Your Goals

Writing down your goals creates the road map to your success. Just writing them down can set the process in motion. Make sure to read and review your goals frequently in order to keep your focus.

Now that you have all your goals, tweak them so they are:

- Specific—describing what you want to accomplish with as much detail as possible.

- Measurable—describing your goal in terms that can be clearly evaluated.

- Finite—stated in terms of time and with a specific completion date.

- Realistic—something you are capable of obtaining.

- Challenging—something that will still stretch you beyond your comfort zone.

Write your goals out in detail. Instead of writing "A new home," write "A 4,000-square-foot contemporary with four bedrooms, three baths and a view of the mountain on 20 acres of land."

Here's the test for specificity: Can you close your eyes and visualize the goal you've written? In the house example, you would mentally walk around the house, look in each room, stand on the porch and see the fog lifting off the mountain. The better you can visualize goals, the more you can program your subconscious mind. And your subconscious plays a huge part in achieving your goals.

If you state goals vaguely, you have a hard time knowing whether and when you achieve them. If you can't measure achievement, you can't measure progress. "Have five new loans by the end of the next month" and "Make $300,000 in commissions this year" are examples of quantified goals.

Setting a time line for a goal is a specialized version of measurability. Specify when you will achieve your goal to help you plan the steps to get there.

Not every wish can be a goal; your goals must be realistic. You obviously want to stay young forever, but you can only cheat mother nature for so long. You must believe you can achieve the goal, or you will not be motivated to try.

And there's this: You must believe, not others. It doesn't matter if no one else believes in you. As long as you believe, anything is possible.

Another thing: Expecting 100% on-target performance of yourself is unrealistic. You will have setbacks and unexpected circumstances. Worse, you may be too hard on yourself and drive yourself unrealistically—leading to demotivation or burnout-related mental and physical problems.

You might believe the goal is possible, but it's not automatically easy or even probable. Being realistic isn't the same as being reasonable.

Still, sometimes you will find enduring value only when you complete the most difficult goals. Keep in mind that some of history's greatest moments were the result of people attempting the "impossible," such as flying or putting a man on the moon.

We can surprise ourselves with what we can make happen when we face exciting challenges. Set goals outside your comfort zone. Stretch your view of reality. That will foster creativity.

On the other hand, not every goal needs to stretch you. Goals that can be achieved right away help build good habits of follow-through and reward you with quick gratification. While challenging goals force you to grow, easy goals reinforce your confidence and motivation. A mix of the two is ideal.

Write down every goal you can think of. Don't worry about how many you have. The more the merrier. Just be creative. Have fun. This is your life—what you want it to be like. No limits.

NEXT STEP: MAKING PLANS

When you have your list of goals in writing, it's time to flesh out the road map to lead you there. Look at each goal and outline the steps needed to achieve it. Asking yourself the following questions can help you to identify sub-goals that lead to achievement:

- What skills do I need to achieve this?

- What information and knowledge do I need?

- What assumptions am I making?

- What resources do I need?

- What help or collaboration do I need?

- What can block progress?

- Is there a better way of doing things?

Revisit the timelines you wrote into the goals. In light of the necessary steps and possible blocks to progress, should you adjust the deadlines?

PUT IT IN WRITING

Words matter, especially when they're on paper. Research shows that people who write out plans succeed more than people who only tell themselves all about it. Putting something in writing makes it more powerful. No wonder society favors written contracts. You can take advantage of this psychological conditioning to help stay motivated: Make a contract with yourself.

In the contract, state your main goals, one from each of the six areas of your life. Then list what steps you will take and when you will complete the tasks. Read your contract every day. If your goals are too small or too large, revise them.

Here's a fun touch in your contract: Include a reward for goal completion. This can help you stay motivated and productive. To make the reward system really work, pick rewards you really want. Large or small, expensive or cheap, if it isn't something you want, it isn't a reward.

Managing Your Goals

Good management of your goals helps you avoid frustration.

- Stay focused. Don't set too many goals to come due at the same time. Don't expect to build a business while getting a law degree while training for a triathlon while raising a family.

- Have at least one simple goal and one difficult goal at any given time. The simple goals motivate you as you accomplish them rapidly. The difficult goals keep you challenged and growing.

- Always have at least one short-term and one long-term goal at any given time. As with simple goals, short-term goals help assure that you'll have frequent victories. Long-term goals (two years or longer) keep you headed in the right direction.

- Prioritize, but be flexible. Decide which of your goals (and tasks) are most important, and assign your due dates accordingly. Be willing to change due dates or even put a goal on hold for a while if necessary.

- Spread out your due dates. Avoid setting a large number of difficult goals with tasks due at the same time.

- Look for ways to combine steps for different goals. If you have a goal to take a vacation and a goal to get better at photography, consider taking a travel photography class that spends a week in the wilderness snapping pictures.

- Strive for balance. Make sure to set goals (whether easy or hard) across different areas of your life. Don't set business goals at the cost of health, friends, and family.

MAKING YOUR GOALS REAL

Get (and Stay) Positive

Our inner voice is always nattering. All too often, what we say about ourselves is pretty negative. But that internal voice can be trained through techniques such as affirmations. Repeating thoughts like "I'm in control" or "I can do it" may sound simplistic, but just think about how often our inner voice tells us "I can't." We should listen to positive thoughts at least as much as we do negative ones.

Write each goal using positive language. Work for what you want, not for what you want to avoid. Part of the reason we write down and examine our goals is to create instructions for our mind to carry out. The more positive instructions you give it, the more positive results you will get.

VISUALIZE

Like positive thinking, visualization is using your imagination for self-improvement. The subconscious doesn't differentiate between real events and imagined ones. If you visualize yourself attaining your goals, your subconscious will process those pictures as if you've actually done them. That makes the goal easier to attain.

GO TANGIBLE WITH PICTURES

The more visual and real you can make the goal, the better it will work. So whatever you are working for, make it visual. Cut out pictures that show your goal. Tape them to a poster board and hang it where it'll constantly be in your face. Same idea when you're on the go. Carry a picture with you so you can see what you are working toward every time you become discouraged or feel like slacking off.

Before Mercedes made their M Class SUV available, I got a picture of the concept model. And it was the most beautiful SUV I had ever seen. As soon as I saw it, I made the decision to save enough money so that by the time the car was available I would have enough saved to buy it in cash.

I kept the picture in my wallet, so that whenever I opened it I would see the picture and be forced to reconsider the purchase I was about to make. Several times, after seeing the picture, I decided I could live without whatever it was I was going to buy. When the car was available, I had almost saved enough. But the sad part was that when they made the car available it was nothing like the picture they had released earlier, so I didn't get the car.

Having the picture there to remind me helped me change my behavior several times.

ACT AS IF

It's obvious body language tells a lot about our mood. Here's a twist: You can use your body language to change that mood. If you act confident even though you feel discouraged, you'll quit being so bummed. You'll get a grip on yourself. The same is true of achieving your goals. Act as if they have been achieved, and you will see opportunities and solutions that may have passed you by before.

I dare you to try being depressed while you are jumping up and down with a big fat smile on your face.

IF THE GOING GETS TOUGH ...

You may start a goal-setting exercise, only to feel over-whelmed by the process. Keep the following guidelines in mind to help you de-stress:

- Where you have several goals, give each a priority.

- Focus on one goal at a time to simplify the process.

- Make sure the goal you are working on is something you really want, not just something that sounds good.

- One goal cannot contradict any of your other goals.

- Make sure your goal is hard enough to excite and challenge you.

- Keep your immediate goals (today, this week, this month) small and achievable.

Prioritizing goals can be confusing if you think in terms of "which is more important?" This is because all of your goals are important or they wouldn't be goals. This is like choosing between breathing and eating. They're both big. OK, at this moment, breathing is more important. But eventually, all the air in the world won't matter if you don't get some food.

Even when one goal laps another, timing sometimes pushes the less important goal to the fore. You know this one: Family might be your most important priority, but sometimes you vault working late over dinner with the wife and kids. It's called reality.

Assume that all your goals weigh the same. Consider abandoning the notion of prioritizing by "importance." Instead, think in terms of timing: "Which needs my focus right now?"

At any given time, you can choose to focus on some goals more than others. The goal that receives the most attention will probably change frequently. This flexibility lets you have fun and set diverse goals such as travel, savings, relationships, and health. You can keep track of them, focusing on certain ones now and shifting focus to others as needed. You can even set a long-range goal with a start date that doesn't begin for several years. At least it will be there to look at when you review your goals and think about the future.

Some people prefer to work on their goals one-at-a-time. That's fine. Others opt to adjust the date settings of each goal (and its associated tasks) to manage multiple goals simultaneously, shifting attention and effort.

Goals can be set too low because of fear of failure. If that's so, you will not take the risks needed for top performance. Don't be scared. As you apply goal setting and see the achievement of goals, your self-confidence should increase, helping you to take bigger risks. Know that failure is a positive thing. It shows you areas where you can improve your skills and performance.

Sometimes we must revise a goal because of an unexpected conflict with other goals. If you need to change a goal, do not consider it a failure; consider it a victory because you grasped the situation.

What about letting others in on your direction? Better to lie low. Unless you positively need someone to help you achieve your goal(s), do not share your goals with others. The negative attitude from friends, family, and neighbors can drag you down quickly. It's crucial that your self-talk (the thoughts in your head) are positive.

FACING FAILURE

Things do not always go as we plan. When you fail to reach a goal, do not give up. Learn lessons from the failure and get back to the process. Remember that by trying something, you see doors open that otherwise would be closed. Failure can hurt. When goal setting goes wrong, the benefits are lost and the whole process can get thrown out, which eliminates a potent tool in your success arsenal.

If you have failed to achieve a goal or see failure looming, see if the reason is in the following list. Use the suggested fix to adjust the goal and create a new plan. Doing your own feedback process turns everything into a positive learning experience. Even failing to meet a goal is a step toward successful performance.

- Goals may rely too much on outside factors. If you fail to achieve a goal for reasons outside your control, this can be dispiriting and lead to loss of motivation. *Suggested fix: Set goals that depend more on your own actions and abilities than on outside factors.*

- Goals can be set too high. When a goal is perceived to be unreachable, it will be abandoned. *Suggested fix: Set goals that challenge you but are not "impossible" in your view.*

- Goals can be set so low that there is no challenge or benefit in achieving the goal. There isn't a good reason to allocate resources to a goal like this. *Suggested fix: Always set goals that are challenging, exciting, and obviously beneficial.*

- Goal setting can be unsystematic, sporadic, and disorganized. They will be forgotten or achievement will not be measured. *Suggested fix: Be organized and efficient in using goal setting and managing.*

- Too many goals may be set, leading to a feeling of overload. *Suggested fix: Stick to two or three primary goals, and remember that you deserve time to relax and enjoy being human.*

Remember: If you set a goal to hit the sun, and you can hit only the moon, that is still something worth celebrating!

KEEPING IT GOING

Once you know your goals, review your list daily. That's a crucial part of your success. Each morning, read your list of goals that are written in the positive. Visualize the completed goals: See the new home, smell the leather seats in your new car, feel the cold hard cash in your hands. Then each night, right before you go to bed, repeat the process. This process will start your subconscious and conscious mind on working toward the goals. This will replace any negative self-talk with positive self-talk.

Every time you have a decision to make, ask yourself, **"Does this take me closer to or further from my goal?" If the answer is "closer to," you can make the right decision. If the answer is "further from," well, you know what to do.**

If you follow this process every day, you will be on your way to achieving unlimited success.

In the long-term, don't focus on the goal so much that you lose sight of the underlying reason you set the goal in the first place. The world changes. While follow-through and persistence are among the most important traits related to long-term accomplishment, so is the ability to reassess. As long as you are honest with yourself, it's OK to change your mind, change goals midstream, shelve one for a later day, or cancel one altogether. The trick is to not change your mind so frequently that you never accomplish anything.

When you have achieved a goal, use the results to feed back into your next goals:

- If the goal was easily achieved, stretch your next goal further.

- If the goal took a dispiriting length of time to achieve, make the next goal easier.

- If while achieving the goal you noticed a deficit in your skills, set goals to fix this.

Remember that goals change as you mature. Adjust them regularly to reflect this growth in your personality and circumstances. If you're not into a particular goal any longer, let it go. Goal setting is your servant, not your master. It should bring you pleasure, satisfaction, and a sense of achievement.

In the mortgage business, things can move very quickly or they can move super slowly. It is easy to get overwhelmed and lose sight of where you want to go. Goal setting is one tool that we use to keep control of our lives and our business.

One important item that I mentioned briefly earlier in this chapter is the power of the subconscious mind. When you constantly think about a goal or a problem, your subconscious finds a way to manifest it.

If you think negative things all day long, those things and more will happen to you. If you think about your goals, your subconscious goes to work and stays at work 24 hours a day, working to find solutions and ways to accomplish your goals.

If you truly desire something, you can achieve it.

In this chapter we use the method of goal setting to clarify the things most important to you in life. We also discovered a way to get your desires on paper and came up with a time frame for when you will accomplish your dreams and achieve what you desire.

Have you written down all your goals?

Do they have time frames?

Are you motivated enough to do what it takes to make these goals and dream come true?

If yes, you are ready to discover the easy way to dominate a market and reap its reward which is conveniently covered in the next chapter.

CHAPTER 2

CREATE AND DOMINATE THE MARKET

WHAT IS YOUR TARGET MARKET?

Is it anyone who wants a mortgage?

If you answered with a yes, you're off the mark. You're working harder and spending more money than necessary to promote your services. And you're enjoying only a fraction of the commissions you should be getting.

Most loan officers recognize the value of targeting a market. The point here is: How big a market should you target? Who exactly is your customer anyway?

When you target a broad audience like "anyone who wants a mortgage," you're targeting prospects who *are able to use* your services. Right now, there are a lot of people who are looking for a mortgage. Are all these people worth going after?

Nope. Just because they are able to use you, does not mean they are going to.

In order for your marketing to be cost effective, you need to narrow your focus to those who are most *likely to use* your services. This means you need to refine your market. In other words, you need to find a smaller sub-set of the whole market. We call this niche marketing.

Market segmentation, boutique services, specialty markets— theses are all terms that refer to *niche marketing*.

Such marketing concentrates on selling to a small, focused portion of a market. This is the opposite of mass marketing, which accommodates as much of the market as possible. Coca-Cola is a product built for mass marketing. That is why they must spend billions every year to keep promoting it. Diet Cherry 7-Up on the other hand, is a niche product because it only appeals to 7-Up drinkers who are watching their weight and like the taste of cherries.

Most companies direct at least some of their marketing to niche audiences. Even the country's largest manufacturers pin-point markets to maximize the effectiveness of their programs. Those firms often target different niches for each product group. Hewlett-Packard markets all-in-one tabletop machines that print, fax, scan, and copy to the home office market. The company also targets large businesses for its larger, faster, and higher-priced units.

Then there's Nike. The multi-billion dollar company soared by pursuing a segmentation strategy. Nike designed and marketed athletic shoes for different sports, often further segmenting with specialized models within each sport (e.g., Air Jordan basketball shoes and additional basketball models called Force, represented by Charles Barkley and David Robinson, and Flight, represented by Scottie Pippin).

Countrywide could be considered a mass marketer. They offer hundreds of loan options and they advertise to everyone looking for a mortgage. But even then, they offer niche products to capture as many customers as they can.

Market niches can be geographic areas, a specialty industry, and ethnic or age groups. Sometimes a niche product can be a variation of a common product that is not produced and marketed by the main marketing firms.

A niche market is a narrowly defined group that includes the following:

- Individuals who have the same specialized interests and needs.

- Individuals who have a strong desire for what you offer.

- Prospects you're trying to convince to do business with you instead of with someone else.

- Prospects you can easily reach.

- Production large enough to fit your needs.

- Action small enough so that your competition will likely overlook it.

WHY NARROW YOUR FOCUS?

Gone are the days of, "You can have it in any color as long as it's black." Lenders offer thousands of loan options. Why? Because people have special needs.

Often loan officers view a niche market as a limit to their sales potential, so they ignore it. They like bragging that they can do any kind of loan under the sun. That's great. But here's the truth: being active in a niche market can make you a ton more money than marketing to the public at large. A niche market lets you define whom you are marketing to. When you know that, it's easy to determine where to spend your marketing energy and dollars.

Take a car dealership. It will certainly sell a car to anyone who wants one, but does that mean its market is anyone interested in buying a car? No. The dealership needs to focus on a geographic market—such as people within a 50-mile radius. So it should communicate to individuals in that geographic area only. Buying ads in newspapers outside their area would be a waste of money.

The dealership could also pursue niche marketing according to the types of vehicles it sells—maybe trucks or only luxury cars. Narrowing the types of vehicles sold also narrows the characteristics of its market.

A niche market lets you target your sales messages with the precision of a darts champion. The more narrowly you define your niche market, the easier you can cater to customer interests.

Since a niche market is small, it lets you get more bang for your marketing buck. Not only that but when you focus on a niche you can become an expert on serving those customers. You can help them overcome their specific problems and concerns better than any other loan officer. And when you can do that, they will tell their friends who are also in that niche and your business will grow from there.

For example, let's say you know Swahili (it's a language), and in your city there is a large concentration of people who speak Swahili. Who would they rather talk to, someone who speaks the same language, or the big bad banker who only speaks English? They will come to you. That becomes your niche. And it is a niche that you can easily dominate, quickly and cheaply.

Often, there are small communities of people who need our services, but there is no bank or mortgage company that offers what they need. Or even if they do, they don't tell the niche.

For example, one of my coaching clients decided to make motorcycle owners his niche. He visited all the bike dealers in his city and told them how he can help them sell more bikes. If one of their customers was low on cash, he could help them get some money out of their house. This loan officer became the unofficial loan officer of the biking community in his city. Every time a biker wanted a bike but couldn't afford it and owned a house, he/she was referred to my client.

Being in a niche also gives you the chance to be seen as the expert. Let's say you focus on condo loans. You become the leading expert in your city on condo loans. You know them in and out. Once you let the world know, they will come to you.

If you were buying a condo, who would you rather work with? A guy that only does condo loans and is recognized in the city as an expert in condo loans, or your sister's new boyfriend who does any loan he can get his hands on? Due to the added complexities of a condo purchase, most buyers will go with the expert. Especially if the expert tells them all the things that can go wrong if they don't use an expert. One just like him.

Specialization also means higher fees. A brain surgeon makes a heck of a lot more than a general practitioner. A trial attorney makes more than a tax attorney. And a specialized loan officer can charge more for his specialized services as well.

RECOGNIZING NICHE MARKETING OPPORTUNITIES

Not much difference exists between a regular prospect and niche market prospect. So loan officers sometimes find themselves in a niche market without planning it. Perhaps friends and family members ask you for advice, help, or a certain kind of service. Do they see you as the expert in an aspect of your business? Can you turn this expertise into a niche?

Not only can niche marketing make you more money, but it can add a lot of fun to your business as well. One of the best ways to identify a niche is to examine the clubs you already belong to, and the hobbies you enjoy.

Today, there are groups, clubs, associations, and gatherings for everything and anything. All of these are small niches.

Let's say you like to fish. Then why don't you focus on people who are just like you and love to fish as well. That can be your niche. You can add fish images to all your stationary. You can advertise in the fish magazines. You can exhibit at fishing trade shows. You can offer a free fishing trip when someone gets a loan from you. That way you get to go fishing a lot more, you get to bond with the new customer, and it's tax deductible! Win-Win-Win!

Later in this chapter, I list dozens of niches that you can focus on.

IDENTIFYING A NICHE MARKET

A well-defined niche should consist of people with the same specialized needs that you satisfy. Your job is to spell out compelling reasons for people in this group to do business with you—and not with your competition. Just make sure the target group is large enough. You want a solid volume of business needed to meet your goals.

Location is crucial as you scratch your niche, but also look for a different slice of the general market. You could target specific property types, particular age groups, or a certain ethnic community. You might focus on first-time home buyers, retirees seeking to downsize their property or secure a reverse mortgage, or buyers with less than perfect credit.

Look at yourself first. What do you like to do and what types of people do you like to hang around with? Let's face it. You relate to people with similar interests. As Robert Cialdini writes in his book, *Influence*, "As a rule, we most prefer to say yes to the requests of someone we know and like." And the easiest way to get people to like you is to have something in common with them.

Did you get that? If you want someone to do what you want them to, it is much easier if they like you. And people tend to like people who are just like them. So when you choose a niche, make sure you have something in common with your niche.

It is not by accident that ethnic loan officers get a lot of business from their own ethnic group. Most people feel comfortable dealing with their "own people". Or at least someone who is like them.

To be successful in your niche, you must know its members intensely: their thoughts, likes, motivations, habits, and lifestyle.

To consider your niche markets, write answers to these questions:

- What do my current clients have in common?

- How do I set myself apart from the competition?

- What is different about the services I offer?

- What extras do I bring to the market?

As you brainstorm for answers, think of what group of people would be most interested and benefit the most from your services. Make a list of potential markets that your answers point to.

Here's another way to find niche market candidates: Work backward from the benefits you offer. List all your services' benefits. Then list characteristics of prospects who would gain by those benefits. You should begin to see narrowly defined groups emerge. These are your niche candidates.

Next up: With your short list of candidates, you can consider each niche in more detailed terms.

If you pick the right market niche, you could be in the money. You just have to select the right factors:

- Measurable in quantitative terms (e.g., dollar volume, average number of buyers).

- Substantial enough to generate planned revenue.

- Accessible to your communication/marketing methods.

Some things to learn about your niche customers: Where they live, where they shop, what they do for fun, what do they read, what places do they visit.

Like a good coach, know the competition. Assess competitors in the market niche and determine how you will position against them. Review their ads, brochures and websites, looking for their key selling points, including pricing and delivery. Think in terms of:

- Strength of competitors to attract your niche buyers away from your services.

- Similarity of competitive services in the niche buyers' minds.

- Ease of entry/protect ability in the market for your niche.

If you see little or no competition in the niche you are considering, don't assume this is positive. True, it may mean other companies haven't found the key to successfully providing a service to this market. It's also possible many companies have tried to penetrate this group and have found that it wasn't what they expected.

Once you have determined the size and competitors in the potential niche, consider how well you match the market:

- What are the unique needs of this niche, and are you capable of meeting them? The benefits you promise must have special appeal to the niche's buyers. What can you provide that's new and/or compelling?

- Are you culturally aligned with the niche? When approaching a new market niche, it's imperative to speak its language. In other words, you should understand the market's hot buttons and be prepared to communicate with the target group as an understanding member of the community—not as an outsider.

The best types of niches are:

- a group of people with whom you have something in common.

- a group who requires some sort of specialized service.

- a group who is being ignored by your competition.

PARETO'S LAW AS A NICHE MARKET

You probably know Pareto's Law, though you may not recognize the name. Translated into business terms, a version of the law states that 20% of your buyers account for 80% of your revenue. That 20%—your heavy users—may very well be your niche market. If you can identify those heavy users and find others like them, you could sell more with much less effort. In this context, niche marketing means targeting, communicating with, selling, and obtaining feedback from the heaviest users of your services.

Think about it. What are the characteristics of your heavy users? Do they have anything in common? If so, do those shared characteristics point to a particular niche that you could pursue?

Are the majority of your loans coming from first-time homebuyers? People from your old job? People with bad credit?

GETTING STARTED

Once you identify the niche market you want to serve, plan to establish yourself. The plan needs to include:

- Your personal and professional goals.

- A general description of the proposed niche, including your qualifications and reasons for pursuing this market.

- Pricing structure.

- Costs of servicing the niche.

- Expected obstacles.

- Required fees or dues.

- Resources, capital, knowledge, skills, and talents that you have for establishing yourself in this niche.

- Any resources you lack, and how you will make up for them.

- A market analysis, including the estimated size of the market in terms of dollar volume.

- Projected revenue schedules and volumes.

- Projected expenses.

- A sensitivity analysis, which estimates the amount of risk you are taking by pursuing this niche and how it can be mitigated.

You will likely need advice and support to establish your niche market. Look for people doing something similar. Find out who is doing what you hope to do and learn from them. Seek reference material from libraries, the Internet, and the news media. In short, network!

Consider the fellow I told you about who marketed to bike owners. He used the bike dealers to get to his ultimate customer. Who can you use that already deals with your niche to recommend you?

MARKETING TO YOUR NICHE

When you have a lead on a niche market, you're out front in becoming a leader in your business area. Now you can maximize your marketing budget by targeting your defined niche market.

How will you get and stay in touch with your niche? Can you join their group and go to their meetings? Do they have a magazine or newsletter you can advertise in?

Cater to your niche market. Write and place articles in media that your prospects follow. Give presentations to organizations that your niche buyers belong to. Be seen as the expert mortgage person in the niche.

Be creative too. Come up with a catchy slogan or moniker. I don't think there is any city that doesn't have some realtor calling himself the "Condo King". But it is catchy and explains the niche right away to prospective clients and referral partners.

FORM A NICHE COMMUNITY AND BENEFIT YOUR BUSINESS

If you can't find a niche, make your own!

Humans need community. We survive and thrive in relationships. We are social beings. Alone doesn't cut it. It's a drag. Ever since we lived in caves, our social environment has determined our fate.

Given that most of us have an unmet need for community, one of the greatest services you can offer your clients and prospects is to get them together.

Think about it. A niche is a group of people who share common situations, needs, and goals. When these people get together, they feel a common bond; they understand each other and can easily provide mutual support.

By creating a niche community, you're suddenly a trustworthy resource. The secret to success is targeting a group of people with specific interests. Any niche you can think of for your service is a candidate for a niche community.

By establishing a niche community around your business, you can enjoy these benefits:

- Increased visibility. Community participation is a low-cost marketing strategy that can yield enormous exposure for your business. Virtual communities provide free or low-cost gatherings that attract more people and create more prospects.

- Increased credibility. The success of your niche community reflects on your abilities as a service professional. It provides a chance for you to show your stuff and impress prospects who don't feel like they need to ward off a sales pitch.

- Word of mouth. Virtual communities stimulate conversation. They get people talking. Participants tell their friends about your business as a community resource than a private service.

By reaching more people through your virtual community, you will develop a platform to sell more services. Your community can open the door to multiple income streams through group mentor programs and information products.

First consider how you will structure your community and bring people together. You have three choices: find a group of people who do not see themselves as a niche but have enough in common to be one, create a live community that meets in a physical location or by telephone; or establish an online community that meets through the Internet.

A perfect example of a niche that is ready for you is a farm. Realtors are masters at this technique. They pick a portion of the city or a subdivision. Usually about 500–1000 homes, and they try to position themselves as the expert realtor in that area.

Live communities make your life easy. Just develop a statement of purpose for your group, then market the group to niche market prospects close to one another, choose meeting times and a location (or arrange a teleconference), and bring them together around a structured agenda. You can use the sessions to educate your niche buyers, or you can help the group discuss issues with each other.

Virtual communities gather people in an online space where they communicate, and get to know each other over time. They can trade information and find support.

The core of facilitation and hosting is to serve the group and assist it in reaching its goals or purpose. Some describe this role as a gardener, a conductor, a teacher, or an innkeeper.

If you take the plunge, be patient. Niche communities don't gel overnight. Often they take time to coalesce into something valuable and sustainable. It's crucial you have patience. Soon enough the community will become established.

Any easy way to create a virtual community is to start a web portal for a community. I have seen realtors do this with great results. They create a website just for a specific subdivision or small city. They list all the happenings in the area. They invite the people living there to post items and announcements. The website brings the community together and the realtor is seen as the sponsor. So when anyone thinks of selling, who do you think they think of first?

THE CHOICE IS YOURS

You can pick from hundreds of niches. Any commonality among people can be called a niche. And since everyone wants to own a home, your services are a hot commodity. So it's a simple equation. By catering to this group, it becomes your niche.

To help you brainstorm possible niches, here are several:

Bankruptcies

Finding the right lender and learning how to package these loans can lead to high commissions per loan. Often, these people have nowhere else to turn for mortgage help. The number of bankruptcies has been soaring the last few years. This is a huge niche that can be very profitable.

Fishermen/Hunters/Golfers

These people are enthusiastic about their hobbies. They spend a lot of time and money on their interests. You can call them addicted. They have their own groups, magazines, gathering spots, and lingo.

These are just three examples. Any other group that exhibits similar traits would also make a great niche. It would help if you were a member of these groups yourself. Affinity goes a long way in creating trust.

Celebrities

Local celebrities live in every marketplace. And several older, retired celebrities probably live around you. These people are used to star treatment and people catering only to them. Establishing relationships through business managers and publishers is a great way to get into this market.

College Students/Parents

Parents might need to take out a second mortgage or refinance to get cash to send Junior to school.

Another sub niche is the trend in parents buying condos for their kids when they go to college. The students live in the condo during school and save on dorm expenses, and the parents have a place to stay when visiting, as well as a tax break for a second home.

A third sub niche is to market to college graduates.

Construction Loans

Construction and bridge loans are a market in themselves. If new homes are going up in your area, then people are building their own homes. A great place to find borrowers is from the builders themselves and from realtors who cater to this niche.

Divorced Couples

People going through divorce must make financial changes. They may need to sell their house or refinance it to get it out of both their names.

FHA

You need to be approved for a Federal Housing Administration loan and the process is stringent, but this can be a great solution for borrowers who do not qualify under the Federal National Mortgage Association.

VA

Veterans Affairs customers are easy to find, and they can buy more quickly since they need no down payment.

First-Time Buyers

These folks are a pleasure to work with. They see the loan officer as sent from heaven. They listen and do what you tell them to do. Best of all, they make great referrers. After they get their house, they can't wait to tell everyone about you.

Workers at a Large Company

By contacting the human resources department of a large company or organization, you can arrange to do home buying seminars or any other type of loan-related seminar.

Condo-Tels

This is a new type of vacation home—a cross between a condo and a hotel. Suites are being sold that include all the amenities of a hotel: room service, doorman, front desk, maid service, etc.

Doctors

They are a professional category. You can just as easily market to other professions: nurses, web designers, software engineers. Show these niches that you specialize in their profession and know what they need.

FSBO

Spelled out, that's For Sale By Owners. This group involves people trying to sell their homes without a realtor. They need your help to qualify the prospective buyers. They will also most likely buy another house and will need a mortgage for it.

Gays and Lesbians

Same-sex unions bring out special problems in originating. You must know the specific problems that can occur and how to package the loan to overcome these obstacles.

Jumbo Loans

These go above the loan limits of FNMA, so you need lenders that handle these loans. These borrowers are typically wealthier than average folk.

Investors

Real estate investors are easy to find, but they usually need to move quickly. Local real estate associations exist in most cities.

Newlyweds

These people are prime candidates that not many loan officers go after. They are good first-time buyers.

Reverse Mortgages

Reverse mortgages are given only to seniors with equity in their homes. You help them cash out the equity so they can live off it and still stay in the house. These loans have received a lot of media attention lately.

Military

Holding seminars at a military base can be highly effective. These people are trained in doing what they are told to do. So they tend to listen very well and turn in all the documents on time. You will have to be familiar with their pay structures and stationing time frames.

Public Servants

These are police, firefighters, federal and local government employees. They sometimes get special breaks—like police officers who get a 50% price break on Housing and Urban Development Department homes in certain areas.

New Immigrants

This group is usually hardworking, and depending on the country of birth, can be highly educated with high earning potential. To work with this group, you will have to be aware of immigration laws and loan programs that cater to those without citizenship.

Ethnic Community

It is much easier to target an ethnic community if you belong to it or at least speak its language. These folks need a lot of handholding if they have just moved here. And keep in mind most groups like to do business with their own.

Professional Athletes

Doing business with one athlete can result in multitude referrals. Athletes are usually young and can use the help of a good professional who looks out for their best interest.

Religious Group

Most religious groups already have a loan officer as a member. So it is best to target only the group to which you belong.

Harley-Davidson Owners

I use this name to mean people who not only belong to a tight-nit group, but who also would take cash out of their house to make a large purchase.

You could also target collectors of art, coins, or even vintage cars.

Commercial

Commercial properties are interesting because each one is different and a different package must be created for each property. But the payday can be a very large one.

Subprime

People with bad credit are not bad people, and they deserve a second chance. Subprime loans are harder to place, and that allows the loan officer to charge more for the loan.

Relo's

Relocation buyers want things to be quick and easy. You can find them through a relocation specialist realtor or the human resources department of major companies in your area.

Second-Home Buyers

This is a great niche in a vacation or resort area.

Self-Employed

The self-employed have more complicated tax returns and cannot always show their true income. That is why they prefer No Doc or Stated loans.

Teachers

HUD has a Teachers Next Door program where teachers get a 50% price break on HUD homes in certain areas.

Home Improvement

Home improvement loans are usually second mortgages or lines of credit that charge a higher rate than the first mortgage.

MORE THAN ONE NICHE?

You can focus on as many niches as you can handle. There is no limit. But you need different marketing pieces and different pitches for each. To be successful in a niche, you should be seen as the expert in that area, or that you cater exclusively to that niche. Having too many niches takes away that exclusivity.

Better to start with one that you're familiar with. Most of my new loan officer coaching clients market to their friends and family first, and their church or religious membership second. Having something to talk about besides mortgages helps break the ice.

Once they become known in their religious organization as a loan officer, they branch out into other niches that they plan to conquer.

This chapter introduced us to the world of niching. Getting a large piece of a small pie is easier to do than getting a small piece of a large pie. Especially when all the big fish are also trying to get the large pie but very few fish are after the small pie.

By focusing on a niche, you can:

- Focus your marketing on those most likely to use your services.

- Be seen as an expert in a chosen area.

– Increase your referrals.

– Have a lot more fun.

– Charge more for your services.

CHAPTER 3

THE MORTGAGE GUY WITH PURPLE HAIR

Here is the million dollar question: "Why should I get my loan from you rather than someone else?" Be able to answer this question and you can have the world eating out of your hand.

Astute marketers have an expression for standing apart: the Unique Selling Proposition (USP).

It's also called: the Unique Buying Advantage, the Value Proposition, or Positioning.

They all mean the same thing.

Every average loan officer has trouble answering the above question. They mumble something vague and general. No wonder people don't want to do business with them.

You must have a USP if you want to stand out from the crowd. You must have one if you want to be seen as a special loan officer and not just another salesman. The USP is what tells prospects why they should work with you instead of everyone else.

If you do not stand out, there is only one way to compete: price. And if you don't already know, competing on price is a losing proposition. We do not compete on price. We find ways to show that we are worth our fees, and prospects gratefully pay what we ask. But only if we are seen as unique.

Your USP must *instantly* tell people why they should do business with you.

Your USP must also be specific, concise, and meaningful.

For our purposes, you must ask yourself further: "Why would someone refer me to his friend or family instead of someone else?"

It's not just about getting that prospect's business. It's about getting all his referral business as well.

UNIQUE SELLING PROPOSITION VS. SLOGAN

A USP is similar to a slogan in that it is a statement you want people to associate with you. It is present in all your advertisements and other promotional material. Finally, it is the one factor that distinguishes you from all the rest. While a slogan generally stops there, an effective USP goes deeper into the mechanics of a business because it can give your marketing pizzazz in the public's eye.

By promoting your USP, you are promising current and potential customers a unique service or special feature. The USP is meant to permeate your entire business structure.

For example, if you promise that every phone call will be answered by a live person during business hours, then everyone who works in your office knows they must courteously answer every single phone call.

When FedEx started, it discovered that customers wanted a reliable overnight service. People did not care how mail reached them or who owned the planes—so long as it got there on time.

FedEx promptly changed its USP and offered its famous "Absolutely positively overnight" promise. This simple change helped FedEx become one of the biggest companies in the world.

"There in 30 minutes or it's free" is the USP that put Domino's Pizza on the map. The company's research discovered that people wanted home-delivered pizza on time. Period. So Domino's stepped on the pedal (literally). Business boomed, making Domino's the leader in home-delivery pizza.

Sure, Domino's Pizza has nothing to do with mortgages. But it does have everything to do with how a winning USP should be written. This USP built Domino's into a pizza empire!

Let's look at what made Domino's Pizza successful.

First, it answered the question: "Why should I do business with them?" Customers responded with: "If I want fresh, hot pizza delivered to me, I will call Domino's."

Second, this USP is specific and meaningful. It does not say, "It'll be there soon" or "It will be delicious." It says you will get fresh, hot pizza delivered in 30 minutes, guaranteed!

Third, it gave a guarantee. If they didn't back up what they promised, there would be repercussions. With the guarantee, customers knew for sure that they would get what was promised.

Can you imitate the Domino's Pizza USP for your business?

If you have met title agents, you know they all promise quality work FAST. They must. If they don't step on it, the deal could fall through. But one Title agent took this concept much further. She branded herself with the image of sneakers. She wore bright, colorful sneakers when meeting real estate agents and loan officers. She had a picture of sneakers on her business card. And she created a USP, "When speed counts, you can count on me." You can bet customers remembered her.

When you tell someone your USP, it should prompt this response: "Really, how do you do that?"

Let's say someone at a party asks you what you do. Instead of revealing your title, tell him your USP. If you give just a job description, that partygoer is not going to say, "Really, how do you do that?" But they will respond that way if you deliver a well-crafted, exciting USP. When he asks for more information, you can tell him how you do your work so well. Suddenly you have another referral source.

Example: "Hi, my name is Ameen Kamadia, and I make the American Dream come true."

"Hi, my name is Joe Blank, and I give people money."

Both of those are much better than, "Hi, I do mortgages."

Do I REALLY NEED A USP?

Definitely! The hardest thing in the mortgage business is to be remembered. Your competitors spend big money trying to get your potential customers and your past customers to come to them. In order to counter them, you must be No. 1 in your clients' minds. The easiest way to do that is through a USP. It makes you stand out. It makes you different.

Imagine a group of teenagers walking by your window. Which one stands out? The one with the purple hair! He's the only one you look at because you have just a few seconds to watch as they pass. The rest all look alike.

That's exactly the point. You want people to remember you—to pick you out from all their other financing options. Keep in mind that you should stand out for a good reason. So don't go dye your hair purple unless your target market likes that sort of thing.

HOW TO DEVELOP YOUR USP

So now lets' focus on creating your USP. The task of choosing ONE characteristic may sound intimidating, especially if you have no indication where to start. There are many things to consider when figuring what to promote as the one quality that makes your firm *the* company for potential customers.

Demographics. What type of people do you want to attract to your company? You can define your potential customers by income, education level, typical types of occupation, geographic location, and family structure. You'll want to create a detailed profile of your ideal customer. "Locally owned and operated" is a demographic USP.

Needs. By defining your typical or ideal customer, you can determine the needs of this group that are not fulfilled by other mortgage companies. "The Reverse Mortgage Experts" is a needs based USP.

Putting it all together. If you've determined that your typical customers are first-time home buyers, you might also see that the mortgage industry must provide clients with clarity throughout the loan process. You could make this your USP: Vow to fully inform your clients of everything they need to know throughout every step of the loan process.

CONSTRUCTING THE MESSAGE.

After you've decided on your USP, you should write it in a crisp, concise statement that clearly informs all clients (and prospects) of your promise. This promise should be memorable and easily associated with your company. It should also be simple, so avoid cutesy or ornate statements. When people need a mortgage company, they should immediately think of this statement and, therefore, your company.

The real secret to developing your Unique Selling Proposition is to first develop your unique positioning of your business. This is called a unique strategic position—the place you occupy in the public's mind. What is your company's dominance? What makes you special to your clients or prospects?

If you do not occupy a position in the public's mind, you have a marketing problem.

A strategic position statement is like a mission statement. You want to explain how you view your company and where it stands in your marketplace.

Nordstrom's is a good example. It's a department store making excellent profit margins while its competition is going out of business. The Seattle-based outfit has taken a Unique Strategic Position of being No. 1 in service. Its USP goes like this:

"Service Above And Beyond All That Is Expected"

It is almost impossible to be the best in all categories. That's why you need to figure out what makes your company unique and what your strategic positioning is going to be. What is your No. 1 calling card or claim to fame going to be?

A hot buzzword in business is "positioning." A sharp take on this concept is in the book *Positioning: The Battle For Your Mind* by Al Ries and Jack Trout. Positioning has been THE marketing philosophy for most successful companies the last 10 years.

But what is it? And how can you use it?

It goes back to this: What place do you hold in the public's mind? If the answer is none, then yes, you have a problem.

If you hold no place or a negative one among people, they are not going to do business with you.

Example of successful positioning:

Sony has been first at innovation. The Japanese electronics manufacturer wants to be first in whatever's next in technology.

Wal-Mart is the store with the cheapest prices, and it won't be undersold. They stamp low price and full shelves in your mind.

WHAT'S THE BEST STRATEGIC POSITION FOR YOU TO TAKE?

This is crucial: The decision to choose a mortgage lender takes place in the mind, often well before any information is even gathered. A survey done by the National Association of Realtors showed that the majority of homebuyers went to only one lender to get their loan. So if you are not in people's minds, they probably won't even find you.

Without a position, you aren't there.

Common examples of positioning are service, speed of delivery, latest technology, guarantees, and lowest price.

Your company probably has carved out a niche for itself. The problem is that too many loan officers do not even realize what the identity of that niche is.

The customers really know best. You must find out from your best customers why they are doing business with you instead of someone else. This will tell you what your real niche or core competency is within your company right now.

If you think you do one thing and your customers think you do another, you must answer these:

- What causes this difference in perception?

- Did your marketing do too good a job advertising your weakness or what you do least instead of best?

- Have you changed the way you do things and haven't let your market know yet?

If your market has the wrong perception because you are marketing the wrong USP, change it!

These are major decisions. Survey your market, track the results of sales, and make changes. These moves are critical to building a HIGH-PROFIT business.

GET INTO THE MINDS OF YOUR PROSPECTS

How do we do that? We find or create our own position and communicate it over and over to the right target market.

Here is something you must keep in mind when marketing your company, and almost no one does:

You Have To Be Perceived By Your Prospects As Being Different From Your Competition!

Rosser Reeves, the man who is credited with developing the concept of the USP, said that an effective USP ad needed to have three elements:

1. Each USP must make a specific proposition. Not just words or window dressing. Each USP must say, "Buy this product and get this benefit."

2. The proposition must be one the competition cannot or does not offer. It must be unique.

3. It must be strong enough to move your prospects to action.

Over the years the list of what makes an effective USP has grown to eight elements. They are:

1. Your USP must offer a Huge Benefit that the prospect will have trouble ignoring. The bigger and bolder, the better.

Example: "Call Geico. A 15-minute phone call can save you up to 15% on your car insurance."

2. Your USP must be different from your competitors. *Example:* Amazon is not just a regular bookstore; it's "the world's largest bookstore."

3. Your USP must be targeted to your niche or target market. You cannot be everything to everybody. It must be relevant to your market.
   Example: FedEx is not the cheapest. It went after people who wanted their package overnight, with no worry about price.

4. Your USP should be short, simple, and easy to remember and understand. If it is too long to remember, no one will.
   Example: "Tylenol, the pain reliever hospitals use most."

5. Your USP must be believable. If people do not believe what you are saying, they will never pay attention. So you need to add credibility with guarantees, testimonials, and specific results.
   Example: "Domino's—hot, fresh pizza delivered in 30 minutes, or it's free."

6. Your USP must get people to act. If you cannot convince them to act, you might lose them forever.
   Example: Circuit City's "If you find a lower price within 30 days, we'll match it plus refund 10% of the difference."

7. Your USP should be the base of your marketing and your business. Once you determine your USP, put it on all your material. Build your business around it. Your USP is your strength. Ride it to the top.

8. Your USP must be economically feasible. You must be able to do what you say you will, and it should not put you out of business to do it. Your niche should also be large enough to provide enough revenue and profit.
   Example: FedEx now uses the USP "The World, On Time." The company grew its business to become a

worldwide shipper. Even though the new USP doesn't have as much kick as the old one, it lets customers know it delivers worldwide, and right way.

Your prospects and clients must see you as having something different—something special that sets you apart from others and gives them a reason to refer you.

Good positioning just finds and communicates what is different about you. What sets you apart from others who do the same work? Determine what makes you unique so the public will know how it will benefit from your business.

Stop for a second and get a pen and paper. Time to construct answers. In determining your strategic position, try to communicate the following things:

Who you are?

What you do?

Why you are different?

How you can benefit your prospects and clients?

You must know these answers if you plan to communicate them to your market. The answers might not jump up at you, and that's OK. That's the point of this exercise.

A lot of differences should stand between you and others doing the same kind of work. If you don't see that gap, then you are not paying close enough attention or you need to invent something unique that others don't do.

Some examples:

- Open weekends and nights.

- Special financing options.

- New breakthrough technology.

- No premium for extra work.

- Loan closed in 10 days.

- You specialize in _____

- Great guarantees.

- Something for FREE.

Next exercise: Write down all the benefits of your company. Remember, a benefit is an answer to your client's question: "What's in it for me?"

"What's In It For Me?"

People will use you only if they will draw some kind of benefit. You must clearly describe that benefit.

Benefits do not include things like:

- We really care.

- Locally owned and operated.

- Friendly service.

- We are No. 1.

They say nothing about what you will do for someone.

You can come up with even more benefits by asking yourself, "What problems are solved by doing business with us?" This step sometimes is hard because you spend your time listing features instead of benefits.

Just remember, a feature is an item or facet of your product or service. A benefit is what that feature will DO for someone.

You need to get used to seeing what people get from using your services or buying from you. What do they end up with? Do you ever get compliments/comments from your clients? How can you translate those into benefits?

You need to keep your focus. Really see things through the eyes of your clients. Listen to what they say about how you solve their problems. Also use their language to describe that uniqueness.

It is crucial that you know the benefits you can give prospects. You must communicate this to them. When you speak to prospects or clients, you must speak in client language. You must have the viewpoint of the consumer and talk in terms the consumer understands.

Think of it this way. If your best client were to tell some-one else why they do business with you, what would they say?

Now write down the answer to the question: How is your business (and how are you) better and different than those with whom you compete?

What does this mean? List all the ways you think you are better than others in your market and what you feel your strengths are. Very few can be good at all things; if you were, no one would believe you anyway. But for now, list all the ways you think you are better.

Keep in mind you want to tell your prospects how you are different than others in your profession without slamming the competition.

If you start saying "and I've done this and I've done that or we do this and that and that, and I've done the next thing ... and I can do all these things for you," pretty soon you are the jack-of-all-trades-expert-of-none.

Look at it from your public's viewpoint:

- Are there ways you give better service than others?

- Are you more experienced in certain areas?

- Are you more personable, with better guarantees or better payment options?

- Do you have better systems?

- Are you better known? Regarded as an expert?

You might think this is too much work. It's not if you want a profitable business. The only reason the public is uninformed about all of these things is because YOU haven't informed them.

Now we are done with most of the research. We are ready to put all this information into a format you can use.

Next Step: Write a paragraph of 20 to 50 words that uses the best differences and benefits from your research. Communicate, without any hype, who you are, what you do, why you are different, and how you can benefit your prospects and clients.

Don't say, "We are the most experienced in town," which by the way is never believed by anyone.

What you want to say is, "We've been delivering quality service for 25 years."

The 25 years is the hidden proof of your experience. People know you must be able to back up the 25 years statement.

Finally, when creating your USP, you want to remember the emotion. Most people justify their purchase with logic. However, they make the purchase using emotions. They want to do business with you. Your USP should state the biggest benefit and most unique benefit your prospects will get from doing business with you.

Now that you have your paragraph, it is time to condense it. Eliminate unnecessary words and descriptions. Your USP should be no more than three sentences. One sentence is the best. Do not stop until you have a crystal clear, concise, powerful USP you can put into action.

Take the time necessary to create a compelling USP that appeals to your prospects and clients. It will become the cornerstone of your business, and it will drive every aspect of your marketing.

QUESTIONS WHILE CREATING A USP

Here's what you can ask yourself from your prospect's perspective:

1. What's in it for me if I do business with you?

2. What is my greatest frustration with doing business with the mortgage industry?

3. What is my greatest concern with your product?

4. What is the biggest thing I hate about getting a mortgage?

5. Why should I choose to do business with you instead of any of your competition?

EFFECTIVE USE OF A USP

To fully implement your USP, you must integrate it into two areas of your company: marketing and operations.

Marketing. This is where a USP is most like a slogan. You must incorporate your USP statement in every brochure, pamphlet, advertisement (print, television, and radio), website, and email that you use to market your company. This will not only tell people of your promise, but also of what they should expect from you as they visit your company. Incorporating the USP into all of your marketing material also helps ingrain it in consumers' minds.

Operations. This is where the USP begins to permeate your company and go deeper than any slogan. Simply making the promise of your USP isn't enough. You also must live, breathe, and eat your USP. The USP is the basis on which you build your business, service, and success. You and all your employees must integrate the USP into all aspects of your service. If you need to, have them practice different ways to do this. It is also important to follow up with every customer and make sure they were satisfied with the service you promised. This follow-up can be a phone call, email, or letter, but most of all it should thank them for doing business with your company.

The whole basis of a USP is you've found a need that you are trying to fill. Some companies make a promise they can't fulfill. Big mistake. The bottom line is don't make a promise you can't keep. If your USP is an impossible (or even improbable) task for your company, it will actually be counterproductive.

With so many mortgage companies offering so many things, it's important to create a plausible USP. It will set you apart from the others and give you a competitive edge when dealing with actual customers.

CHAPTER 4

THE SECRET TO EVERLASTING SUCCESS IN THE MORTGAGE BUSINESS

What is the mortgage business's one overriding secret? Probably this: Total Client Value (TCV). Understand what TCV is, and you will never do business again the same way.

WHAT IS TCV?

Total Client Value is simply the amount that each client is worth to you.

We routinely hear horror stories of loan officers ripping borrowers off with predatory lending or huge fees. The loan officers who resort to those tactics do not understand TCV. And that is sad because they could make a lot more money honestly, than by trying to hurt people.

Simply put, TCV is the amount of the first commission from your client, plus the lifetime commissions from that client plus the commissions from any referrals from that client. In a short time, this can add up to a very large number.

For example, my average TCV is $11,000. Every time I get a new client, I know that I just put $11,000 in my bank account. I don't have it yet, but it's coming.

A loan is not a one-time transaction. If you treat it as such, you will never form a relationship with the borrower. And that results in cutting yourself off from 90% of your potential profit. So don't stop at the first sale.

Here is why: It costs from ten to sixteen times more to generate a new client, than it does to sell to an existing client. The existing client already knows and trusts you. Especially if you provided Amazing Service™ and stayed in touch.

The hardest part of the mortgage business is generating new clients. This is also the most expensive part of the business. It costs a lot of money to get people to trust you. We as consumers are bombarded by advertising messages every day. And the mortgage industry is one of the leaders in amounts spent on advertising. You cannot turn on the TV, open your mail, or surf the web without mortgage ads popping up all over the place.

And all that money is spent just to generate a lead. Then the lead needs to be contacted, informed and followed up with. And most leads do not materialize into loans. Generating new clients is a very expensive proposition.

That's the bad news. Here's some good news: You do not have to spend nearly as much to sell an existing client. As you build your client list, the majority of your profit should come from repeat sales to existing clients. And if you treat them right, old clients will be happy to refer new ones to you. And when that happens, you have no acquisition cost for that new client.

What do I mean by acquisition cost? That is the money you spend to get a prospect to buy from you the first time. Say you decide to do a letter campaign to an apartment complex. There are 5,000 apartments and you spend $1 per letter. So you spend $5,000. From those letters, say you get 5 responses, and out of those you get 2 loans. You had to spend $5,000 to identify the 5 people who were interested in a loan. And after they raised their hands telling you they were interested, you had to convince them to do business with you.

What if you now wanted to continue marketing to those 2 people who just got their loans from you? Will it cost you $5,000? No way! You could spend less than $1 a month to make sure you stay in their conscious mind so that when they are ready to refinance or move, they will come to you when it's time to get the mortgage. Your net profit (the money you get to keep from your business) will almost always be higher when you market to existing clients.

This brings us to a crucial point. What's the purpose of business?

The purpose of your business (any business) is to make money. The only way we do this is by acquiring new clients and earning more from existing ones. I hope you are in this business for the long-term, that you are committed. Because if you are, and if you understand TCV, then you can achieve amazing success. But it doesn't come right away.

My vision for you is for you to have a business where you have so many existing clients, that you generate as much business as you want from your existing clients coming back to you and from their referrals.

Currently, I do not take new clients unless they were referred from an existing one. All new comers get sent to another loan officer in the office. That is what I want for you. The ability to have more loans than you want without having to spend any money on advertising to generate them.

THE SPHERE OF INFLUENCE

You must focus on long-term relationships with your clients, not short-term, one-time only loans. This may seem like a subtle point, but it is critical, and you must understand it. Too many loan officers measure their success by monthly commissions. They fail to take into account how many new clients/prospects they add to their database, how many clients they market to, and how often they choose to market to them.

The #1 biggest key to success in this business is: *Keep the contact information of everyone you know.*

This is a fundamental concept. If you have 5,000 existing clients and contacts to market to, you will make more money month in month out than if you only have a list of 500. You can control the amount of business you do each month by staying in contact with your client list. This should be your obsession. You shouldn't let anyone who calls, comes in, or inquires about a loan to get away without capturing his contact information.

The Sphere of Influence is a fancy way of saying database. Your sphere is made up of people you have some influence over. It is your friends, family, co-workers, acquaintances, and everyone you know that might do business with you, including past and possible clients.

The first step to building your sphere is to make a list of everyone you know. Take an hour or so and just go wild writing down the names of everyone you know or knew in the past. Make sure to include people your family knows. At this point do not second guess yourself by not listing people who you "think" will not do business with you. You will finalize the list later. For now, put them on the list.

Your goal is to have at least 300 names. When you finish, go through the list and assign each name an letter, A, B, or C.

Those who you are sure will do business with you and give you referrals get A's. Those who you think will, get B's. And those who you do not think will get C's. Go through the C's and see if there is any way to salvage the relationship so they can become B's. If not, then eliminate them.

Once you are done, gather as much information on these people as you can: contact info, work habits, likes and dislikes, hobbies, etc. The more you know, the more you will have something to connect with them about.

Why do so many businesses get in trouble? They fail to get the names and addresses of their clients. Even if they do, they do not communicate with them at all.

In the refinance boom of 2003 and 2004, all we had to do to get a loan was go through our client files and call our past clients. Since the rates had dropped so much, everyone wanted to refinance. It was simply a matter of calling them and setting up appointments for them to come in. They already knew us, liked us and trusted us. For our clients, refinancing with us was a no-brainer. If we had not kept accurate records, we would have lost hundreds of loans!

The Key to Making Yourself Very, Very Rich is an Active and Growing Database!

Are we clear yet? You must add new names to your database and continually market to it. That's the focus of your business.

Everything else is secondary. That is not only how you generate referrals but get your clients to keep coming back as well.

Let's face it, if you do not stay in touch with your clients, they will forget you within 6 months. After a year they won't even remember your name. But if you constantly contact them, they will not only remember you, but you will cement the relationship further.

One caveat: Make sure you separate the names of clients from those who have not done business with you yet. Clients are much more valuable than inquiries. You can make money on general names, but client names are gold. They have backed up their interest in your service with their wallet.

Remember the components of TCV: The first sale to a new client + the lifetime sales to that client + the number of referrals from that client.

First sale: This will always be your most expensive. You might even lose money on this sale, but still come out ahead in the long run. Let me make this clear: I like to make a profit on every loan and believe you should too. But if you are well bankrolled (like Columbia House—10 CDs for $1), it makes sense to go negative on the front end. The point is, your profit will always be much smaller on the first sale compared with repeat commissions. Yet 85% of loan officers concentrate on the first loan and ignore the repeats.

Lifetime Client Value: This is the amount of commission each client generates over his lifetime of doing business with you. It may be a lifetime of 3 years, 10 years or even 20 years. Obviously it is in your best interest to maximize the time this client does business with you. As you get more and more clients and analyze their behavior, you will be able to come up with an average dollar value for the amount your client will spend—including future commissions. The point is this: If your lifetime value of the average client comes to $20,500, then each time you acquire a new client, you have just put an average of $20,500 in the bank. It's not there yet, but it will be as your client goes through your system. It is a nice feeling to have a new client and know you just put $20,500 extra in the bank. Sure, you still have to earn this money. But it is there, and that's what this concept is all about.

Referrals: The best kind of client is one who refers. The second best kind is a referral. Why? You should know this already, but let's recap. Because there is no cost per lead with referrals, and the cost per sale is simply the cost of processing. Referrals can be charged more because they trust their friends and are a source of even more referrals. Treat your referrals with the utmost care and respect. A lot of businesses have been built and a lot of people have gotten rich solely on referrals. This is our intent, too.

All of these together comprise TCV—and you must make maximizing TCV the primary focus of your business. TCV is a cycle: get new clients, do multiple loans for the same client, ask for referrals, sell more to referrals, and ask the referrals for referrals. If you are new to the business, it will take time to build up your database to the point where you can live off referrals. But once you get the process down, you can just insert the clients into the system and let it run.

NUMBERS CAN CLARIFY WHAT THIS IS ALL ABOUT

According to the National Association of Realtors, the average family moves every seven years. Let's say the median price of a house in your area is $160,000. My personal numbers show my clients move every five years and my median home price is $175,000. Your numbers will vary depending on where you live and the economic climate.

If we have a couple that is buying a house and they are both 30 years old, let's see how much they can be worth to you. We will use the median house price of $160,000.

On a $160,000 loan, let's say you make just 1% origination, so that is $1,600. Not bad, but it is just a start. Seven years from now they will be moving into another home, probably bigger and more expensive—let's say $200,000. One percent origination on that will be $2,000. At age 44 they will move up again to buy a house worth $250,000. So that's $2,500 more in fees. And at age 51 they will move to a better neighborhood in the price range of $300,000, so that's $3,000 more. Then they will retire and move to Florida. So in 21 years, this couple will generate at least $9,100 in fees.

That is what you made from just them. If you keep in touch with them and continue to offer great service, you should get several referrals from this couple. Let's say they keep to themselves and are not great at giving referrals. So they send you only one per year. They were your clients for 21 years. That's 21 loans they sent you. If you make only $1,600 per loan, that's $33,600 in fees. Plus the $9,100 you made equals $42,700.

If that is typical, every client of yours is worth $42,700. So is every potential client and every referral. And we haven't counted fees from refinancing. That could double your net value of your clients. Also, one referral a year is low. I have some clients who average two referrals a month.

When dealing with client databases and spheres of influence (everyone you know), the numbers can grow exponentially. If you have 100 past clients, you can bet that 10% of them will move every year. That is 10 possible loans a year for you. Each of these 100 people also knows at least 100 other people each. And 10% of them will move every year. If your past clients are fanatical about referring you, that equals 1,000 potential loans every year!

100 clients x 100 people each = 10,000 x 10% = 1,000 loans

1,000 loans x $1,600 average commission = $1,600,000 in fees

NOW IS THE TIME TO FIND YOUR OWN TVC

First we need to determine what your average commission is. Take the last 20 loans you have done and average out your commission. If I walked into your office today for a loan, about how much would you make from me?

Now find out how many clients you have in your database—the total number of people you have done loans for.

Multiply the two together to determine the value of your database.

If you have 100 clients and you make $1,500 on each loan, your database is worth $150,000. If you implement the strategies taught in this program, you will increase referrals and jack up repeat client business.

So let's say that after implementing a referral marketing system, you get one referral from each client every year.

That equals 100 loans in year one, or $150,000 in income. Now you have 200 people in your database. In year two you receive 200 referrals—$300,000 in income and 400 people in your database. Year three brings 400 referrals, $600,000 in income and a database of 800. And this is all without any marketing to attract new clients off the street. Do you see how powerful this technique can be?

A hitch is that you will not get one referral from every client. But that's not really a problem. Some will give you a lot more than one. Eighty percent of your referrals will come from 20% of your database. As you keep increasing your database, you keep increasing the number of referrals automatically.

Let's be a lot more conservative. Let's say that it takes five years to get 100 referrals. And that in those five years, everyone in your database refinances or buys another home. So essentially you get three loans from each of your 100 clients: the original loan, a refinance/purchase, and a referral.

Your total income would be $450,000. Divide that by 100 clients and you get $4,500.

That is the TVC of each of your clients. Keep in mind that this number is a conservative number. Now that you have the formula, you can determine your own TVC. If you are new to the business and do not have any clients or have not done any loans, safe numbers to use are:

- Average income per loan: $1,500

- Average referral per client: 3

- Average years client stays a client: 8

- Average transactions per client in eight years: 2.5

Using these averages, your TVC per client would be $8,250, and each client will stay with you eight years.

Needless to say, the larger your database, the more you make. If each client is worth $8,250 over eight years, we can assume you will make $1,031.25 per client per year. One hundred clients in your database would be an income of $103,125.

CHAPTER 5

MAKE THE MOST OF THE MOST VALUABLE ASSET YOU HAVE

What is the one asset you can never recoup once you use it? Time. Essentially, time is life. When we run out of time, that's it—you're dead.

How much is your time worth? Do you even know?

We spend so much of our daily time on mundane things. And that time vanishes. How many times do you catch yourself saying, "If I only had more time!"? We all do. And so this chapter is here to help you manage your time more effectively.

I won't tell you how to live your life or bore you with a generic time management seminar. You've no doubt been to one already.

But time management for loan officers stands out. Other people get paid no matter what they do. We do not. If we waste too much time at the coffee shop, that is time diverted from prospecting for our next loan. That is why this chapter is so important. It might seem out of place in a business marketing book, but until you master time management, you will never accomplish what you need to succeed in this business.

How many hours a day do you work? Eight, nine, more? Out of those hours, how many are truly effective, where you are increasing your business, doing an activity to help you grow and earn more? Count up all the hours you waste during the day: all driving time, break time, nonproductive meeting time, phone interruptions from home time, coffee time, newspaper reading time, checking mail and email time, and all other time spent on activities that are not generating income for you.

A *USA Today* survey found that high-paid CEOs say they spend only 50 minutes of each day effectively. They spend the rest of the day putting out fires, with interruptions, and in unproductive meetings.

Examine what you did today and see how many hours were productive. If they totaled more than one-third of the workday, consider yourself lucky.

Now take that number (productive hours) and see how much your time is really worth.

How much do you want to earn this year? Let's say $100,000.

If you work 40 weeks a year, five days a week and eight hours a day, that equals 1,600 hours. If we assume only one-third of that time is productive, in order to earn $100,000 you need to produce $188 per hour.

Seems incredible, huh? But not impossible. If you average $2,000 in fees per loan, you have 10 hours to get, process, and close a loan. From start to finish you can spend only 10 hours per loan. Seems reasonable to me. If you are spending more time than that per loan, you are doing something wrong anyway. The trick is to make sure you have enough loans to work on.

And the only way to get more loans to work on is to get more leads. But you have no time to get leads because all your other time is being wasted on nonproductive things. That is the first thing to change.

Here is the secret of this lesson:

In order to be more successful, you must spend more time on things that bring in money.

Got it?

No magic secret will bring borrowers to you. No matter what marketing tools you use, you must spend time and effort to be successful. Remember this:

"If you always do what you've always done, you'll always get what you've always gotten."

Here's another secret to making money:

You must do at least one thing every day to bring customers in the door.

Simple, but soooo effective.

What makes you money? Customers? Nope. Marketing!

Without marketing, you would have no customers. Every day you MUST take at least one marketing action to attract customers. This is the No. 1 reason people do not get ahead. They do not continue to do marketing.

I have seen this scenario constantly: A broker runs a marketing campaign, maybe by direct mail or radio show. He gets a few leads, and while he is tracking down those leads and turning them into loans, he stops doing the campaign. So after those loans close, guess what? He has nothing in the pipeline!

It doesn't matter how busy you are. You must take out time every day for marketing.

You must also take time for self-advancement: courses, books, and tapes. You either get better at what you do or you get worse. There is no standing still. The only way to get better is to learn. Sure, you get on-the-job training every day, but loans get routine. After a couple of years you know the drill: application, credit, rate, loan package, conditions, set up closing, get check.

Unless you read about the industry and how to improve your business and yourself, you will fall behind.

Just look at the Internet. When it hit real estate in the late 1990s, real estate agents swore they would never use email or the Web. Well, guess what? If you didn't learn to use email or how to put up your own site, you are already out of business or will be soon.

One of the products we are working on at my company is an Assistant Program: showing how to hire, train, and work with an assistant. Of the most successful people, 85% in any business have assistants. Most people think they have assistants because they are successful. WRONG! They became successful because they got an assistant.

Here's why:

If you run a mortgage office alone, you have to do everything: answer the phone, make coffee, take loan apps, market, process, deal with vendors. A simple marketing campaign and two or three loans, and you're swamped; 60–70 hours a week easy. So you hire an assistant—even if you cannot afford it at first. The assistant does all the stuff you shouldn't be doing: answering calls, processing, coffee, you name it. You do what you get paid for: getting loans. So instead of working 60–70 hours, your workload is now 15–20 hours a week. That leaves you with 20 hours to surf the Internet, right? Wrong. You have time to DO MORE MARKETING.

MORE TIME SAVING TECHNIQUES

How about keeping a time log?

Attorneys and accountants keep a time log. James L. S. Collins, president of Chick-fil-A, has been using time logs for years. He knows how crucial they are. Just write down what you do for three days. At the end of the third day you can tell exactly how much time you spent productively versus on things you could have delegated or even worse, not bothered with. Do you know the average household has the TV on for an average of 7 hours per day? How much time do you spend watching TV? Your time log will tell you this and a whole lot more.

Use Your Office

When meeting someone for lunch, meet in your office. If he/she is late, you can keep working until he/she shows up.

Work From Home

Work from home if possible and as much as you can. It saves commute time and interruptions. All you need is a computer and an internet connection. You can easily swap files from home to work with a portable USB drive. Add a fax machine at home and you are all set.

Join the 5 o'clock club.

Mary Kay talked about the 5 o'clock club. Many of Mary Kay's sales associates are women with children and heavy routines of housework and child care. In order for them to get all their work done, they are advised to join the club. You can join, too. All you have to do is wake up at 5:00 a.m. It requires a lot of discipline, but it has many advantages. Much more peaceful. NO interruptions. You can use the office computers without waiting, use the fax and copy machines, answer emails, do all your correspondence, and plan your day. This is a great tip, but not for everyone. I could never get up before the sun. It's not in my nature. Even 7:00 a.m. is too early for me. But if you can, do it. It's worth it.

Learn to speed read.

We all have to read a lot of material to stay current in this business. The faster you get through it, the more time you have for other things. Learning to speed read might be your answer. Get a book from the library or bookstore. Take a class or buy a computer program. For less than $100 you can double or triple your reading speed.

Phone techniques

Phone tag is a big problem. Call a client, he's not in. He calls you back, you are on the phone, and on and on. Here's a simple way to handle this if you have a secretary. If you are on the phone and a call comes in, have your secretary write down the name of the caller. You can decide right there if the call you are on is more important than the call coming in. Indicate that you want the new caller to hold by putting up one finger. Raise two fingers if your current call will take a while.

Whenever someone leaves a message, have him give a time you can call back. Set up your voicemail like this: "Thanks for calling. Please leave your message and the best time for me to call you back." If you can't call at that time, leave a message that you will be unavailable at that time so you called earlier.

Know what you are going to say before you call. Make notes to yourself about the conversation you want to have. Don't waste time talking about the weather or the local sports team unless it helps bond with the other person. Just because the other person has time to waste doesn't mean you do.

Read

Jim Cathcart, a national speaker and salesman, tells this story. In 1972, he was a struggling salesman. Then he heard a radio program by Earl Nightingale in which Earl said, "If you'll spend one extra hour each day in the study of your chosen field ... you'll be a national expert in five years or less." Cathcart reports that "Within five years, just as Nightingale had told me, I was traveling the nation speaking, training, and writing on my chosen subject." Notice that "extra" hour a day. That is above and beyond what you already spend. This works so well because no one else does it. Most people in our field put in normal hours and call it a day. Up until a few years ago, there wasn't even much reading material available on the mortgage industry. Since then, mortgage knowledge has exploded. Several magazines, training programs, and marketing programs can help you. Spending an extra hour does not exactly save you time in the short run. But in the long run, people will seek you out for answers. Customers no one else can help will turn to you. You will be seen as the expert, and results will come. Knowledge is like water behind the damn—power waiting to be released.

Think like a politician.

That's not a typo. Politicians are great at time management. They receive thousands of call, letters, and cries for help, and they can't handle them all. They don't ask, "Which call came in first?" They ask, "Which call is from the most important person?"

So they have to prioritize. All calls to your office are not equal. Take calls first from people who can help you and people who can hurt you. Make sure to identify certain people as VIP. Give these people priority. Calls from others can wait or do not even have to be answered.

Get caller ID.

This goes along with the above time saver. Just because the phone rings does not mean you must answer it. Let the machine get it. This one point is so vital. The ringing of the phone is like Pavlov ringing the bell. As soon as a phone rings, people drop what they are doing and rush to answer. The worst time to do this is when you are with a client. Show your client that they are important to you by ignoring the ringing phone. Whoever is calling can call back.

Don't lose stuff.

Nobody wants to lose anything. But we all do. And a lot of time is wasted looking and searching, not to mention replacing the items lost. Take steps to avoid absentmindedness:

1. Have a place for everything. Don't leave stuff lying around. A place for everything and everything in its place.

2. Write your name, address, and phone number on all important items like your planner and briefcase. And mention a reward if lost.

3. Properly and legibly label all folders, files, and papers.

4. Keep multiple copies of important documents. Have copies of car insurance in your wallet/purse and the glove box. Life insurance and other personal documents should be filed at home and one other place in case your home catches fire. Computers should be backed up regularly, and the backup should be kept in a different location than the computer.

Don't read

"Some books are to be tasted, others to be swallowed, and some few to be chewed and digested: that is, some books are to be read only in parts, others to be read, but not curiously, and some few to be read wholly, and with diligence and attention." – *Francis Bacon.*

Great advice, and it doesn't just pertain to books. Don't waste time on things that are not worth doing. There is no written rule that every book you start and magazine you buy must be read. Yet countless people feel guilty about starting and not finishing. If you are one of them, know this: It's not the end of the world. Put it in perspective.

Good enough is good enough.

Perfectionism wastes time. Writing a letter to a client is one example. You can write a letter in a few minutes or you can take forever to perfectly craft and elegantly compose a literary masterpiece. Will it make any difference to the client? Maybe, but was it worth the time? Nope.

Then there are fax cover sheets. Sure, they look nice and help the person getting it know what the fax is about. But chances are the person knows anyway. The majority of faxes don't need cover sheets. We have more than one lender who faxes rate sheets every day with a cover sheet. That's two sheets of paper for one rate sheet. As if we couldn't tell whom the rate sheet was from.

Beware of Parkinson's Law

Parkinson set out to analyze why large organizations became bloated and lethargic. He came up with this observation: "Work expands so as to fill the time available for its completion." He also stated, "The thing to be done swells in importance and complexity in a direct ratio with the time to be spent."

Deadlines

Some fiction writers today have a new book out every month. Or so it seems. How do some writers write so much, when it takes others several years to write just one book? Deadlines. That is the secret of the journalist. Without deadlines, there would be no newspapers or magazines. Jazz great Duke Ellington once said, "Without a deadline, I can't finish nothing." If you do not place deadlines on your work, it will take more of your time than it should.

Closings

Here is a controversial tip. Do NOT go to closings. As a mortgage broker, I have been to only one closing, and that was my first. I thought I was going to support the borrowers, to make sure they did not get taken advantage of and to show my importance. Actually, I looked and felt like a fool. It took two hours, and there was nothing for me to do. The title agent handled everything so smoothly that all I did was sit there with a smile on my face the whole time.

Many brokers will tell you it is your duty to go to every closing. And that closings never go smoothly. That's baloney. If you have a good team, processor, lender, and title company, things go very smoothly. You are simply not needed.

Sure, I have had closings that did not go smoothly where the title agent had to call me at the office and needed something. But guess what? It was better that I was at the office so I could get her what she needed myself, instead of calling the office and having a processor get it. During a closing, your best position is at your headquarters—your office. That's where all the papers are and where everyone knows to call you. Eighty percent of the time I never hear anything from the title company's people except that the closing was fine and that they are sending the check. So save yourself the time by not going to your closings.

77.9

Do you know what that number stands for? According to the CDC, 77.9 is the average life expectancy for a person living in the United States. How much do you have left?

Subtract your age from 77.9. That is how much you have left (unless you have an accident or get sick). Of course, you could live longer. But this is the average. Twenty percent of your remaining time is lost to eating, sleeping, and going to the bathroom. Ten percent more is lost to shuffling papers, paying bills, and waiting in lines.

If you are in the baby boom category, you have less than 20 years left. In that time you need to work, build up your business, make enough to retire, and whatever else. After all that, that's when you get to stop working and enjoy life.

Unless you start doing it now. Learn these time management skills. Take them seriously. And you will enjoy life much better.

Before a vacation.

So how do you become super productive? Accomplish more in one day than in weeks? Easy. Pretend you are going on vacation.

The day before vacation is easily the most productive day for everyone. Everything important gets done. Time-wasting activities get put aside. Things are checked and placed in order. Desks are arranged. Priorities are worked on and everything else is left for later. That's how it should be all the time. Priorities come first. Paper shuffling comes last. So if you want to be more productive, take more vacations. You will feel more relaxed and refreshed, plus get more done the day before you leave.

Time Blocking

People ask me all the time, "Ameen, how do you find time to run three companies, write, lecture, and consult with people?" The answer will be longer than you care to read. Mainly it is discipline. There are certain things I must do every day whether I want to or not. Sure, I could put them off, but then I would be the one suffering.

One of the things I must do is write. I set aside one hour daily to write new projects: books, newsletters, courses, anything new that must be written. I also set aside time every day to answer emails, read, and return phone calls. Every day is planned in advance. The first few hours are spent doing the everyday items listed above. Then the majority of the day is spent on a major item that has been pre-planned.

I do certain things on certain days. On the first and third Thursdays of every month, I write my Millionaire Loan Officer Newsletter. Every day of the month (except weekends) has a planned priority. On those days, I must concentrate on that priority. Days have been set aside for consulting, for marketing, and for going to the office. With over a dozen projects going on at the same time, this is the best way I have come up with that helps me get everything done on time.

To sum up my personal work schedule:

- Every day of the month has its own major project.

- I also do certain things every day.

Of course, emergencies can pop up and things take longer than the time I planned them for. So I make do. I learned that perfection is impossible. It is better to get something done than never to finish it at all.

My schedule requires a lot of delegation. For the publishing company, Kamrock, I do none of the shipping or customer service replies. Someone else takes care of that. For my rental properties, I don't fix the air conditioning and broken windows. I get contractors to do that.

I want to re-emphasis a point here. Spend time doing what makes you the most money. There is a real estate investment lecturer who has a line, "The less I do, the more I make." At first, it didn't make sense. But the more I thought about it, the more it appealed to me.

Think about it. The less grunt work you do—taking applications, answering phones, driving around to meet borrowers—the more time you have for the most important thing: generating and converting leads.

The E-Myth

A must read book is *The E-Myth Revisited* by Michael Gerber. It is mainly for small businesses and how they can succeed. It details how to go about delegating so you can spend your time on the most important matters. If you heard the line "Work on your business, not in your business," this is where it comes from.

We have already discussed how much you need to make every hour count to reach your goals. If you process your own loans, you cannot be paid more than a processor. If you deliver your own files to the lender, you earn the same as a courier. And that is not very much.

In his book, Gerber talks with a lady who owns a bakery in the mall. She bakes the pies herself, cleans up herself, runs the register herself, and does the books herself. And she is wondering why she cannot get ahead. Gerber shows her that she did not get into business to do everything herself. She got into business because she enjoyed baking and wanted to have a life. So Gerber taught her how to document all the activities that she did not want to do. She wrote down every action taken to clean the ovens, counters, and selling space. She documented what to say to customers and how to give change. She documented how the pies were baked, from gathering the ingredients to cutting the fruit to baking times.

Basically she created a blueprint of every aspect of the business. And then she hired someone. Part time at first. This person was given a written list of everything she was supposed to do: step-by-step. This freed the baker to spend more time on increasing the product line and marketing. Business got better, and the part-time person became full time. Soon, another person was hired. The baker gave the new person his own responsibilities and step-by-step lists on how to perform them.

This allowed the bakery to run without the owner. The two employees knew what to do and did it exactly as if the owner were doing it herself. Maybe not as perfectly, but good enough.

That is the McDonald's formula. Every action should be documented so a part-time high schooler can do it. That is how you have more time to do whatever you want and how you can expand your business. The baker was able to then open more bakeries in other malls. Following this method, you can have people doing everything you shouldn't be doing. And they will do it, just like you would. That frees you to perhaps open your own or a second office.

You might think you must be there to handle the clients. An owner always takes more care in the business than an employee. But the less you do, the more you can make.

To show this works, consider a Remax realtor in Canada by the name of Craig Proctor. This man followed the Gerber system and set up his real estate office. He now has eight assistants and sells more than one house a day! He almost never meets any of his buyers or sellers. The assistants do it all. He focuses on getting people to call his office. He personally has not sold a house in years, but he makes more money that 99% of the agents in Canada.

Procrastination

Every time management lecture requires the mention of procrastination. We all deal with it. And it is the No. 1 complaint people have about their own time management.

We have all heard the normal ways of dealing with procrastination: just do it, focus, take it one bite at a time. If it were that easy, we would never procrastinate. So maybe there is something more to it. Maybe it is more psychological than we thought.

While researching for this chapter, I came across a book by Neil Fiore called *The NOW Habit"* Fiore writes that procrastination is more mental than physical and that we need to understand why and how we procrastinate in order to stop. I am the first person to try to stay away from psychological mumbo-jumbo. But the more I read into his theory, the more it made sense for me personally.

Fiore came up with this definition: "Procrastination is a mechanism for coping with the anxiety associated with starting or completing any task or decision."

So when we have to do something we do not want to, procrastination is a temporary mental release from that anxiety. It is a habit that we learn. By practicing it, we reward ourselves by feeling less tension and take us away from something we see as threatening or painful.

Procrastination has three main benefits:

1. It can express resentment. If you are powerless in a situation, it gives you a sense of control. If you have worked under someone and are assigned a task you do not want to do, procrastination kicks in, lets you drag your feet and do a half-hearted job. It shows your resentment toward your boss forcing you to act against your will.

2. It can defend against fear of failure. Psychologists say this is the No. 1 reason people do not succeed in life. By maintaining high standards and no room for mistakes, you set yourself up for failure. Knowing it is difficult to accomplish your task by your standards, you just put it off. Low self-esteem also pays a huge role here.

3. It can keep you from facing your fear of success. If you succeed and all you see in front of you is more work or a tougher assignment, you won't want to finish. I identify with this myself. I am so good at planning and goal setting that I have goals to write several more books and courses. The list of books to write is three times as long as the list of books I have already written. Yes, I like helping people and that is why I

write, but I don't see an end in sight. As soon as I finish one, I move on to the next, and the next. So now I don't feel like writing at all. At least not as much.

It is the same with athletes and actors. They give their best and get rewarded. But then they are asked to do and give even more, again and again. It is a never-ending cycle. In order to maintain a pace they can sustain, they turn to drugs and stimulants. Instead of the drugs, they could procrastinate. But then they would lose their job, fans, and money.

Procrastination is a mental habit we have learned over the years. We can overcome it by making work more enjoyable and getting more fun out of our leisure time.

Fiore's book goes into many techniques to overcome procrastination. I am just going to highlight a couple here. But if what you have read so far has intrigued you and procrastination is a serious problem for you, get this book. It has helped me and can probably help you as well.

The easiest way to change our thinking is to change our speech. By changing our words, we change the meaning associated with them and change the way our body and mind react.

Procrastinators talk in "have to's" and "should do's"—"I should do this, but I don't want to." "I have to turn this report into my manager by Wednesday or I will get fired." These statements take the power out of our hands and make us feel helpless. They create feelings of pressure from outside sources and of lost control. These words tell our minds that we are in a no-win situation and that we do not have any choice in the matter. The "have to" statements elicit stress, and the "should do" statements create depression.

Taking back control of the situation begins with changing your words. Instead of "have to" or "should"—say "I choose to" even if you don't. I do not know why, but just using the words "I choose to" makes me feel lighter and less stressed. Maybe since I choose to do something, I can choose not to do it in the future if I don't want to. It's amazing how it works.

Other options:

Instead of negative thinking "I must finish"
you can say "when can I start?"

By changing the focus on the future to what is in your control, you can start getting things done. Any action taken is better than no action.

Instead of negative thinking "This is so big"
you can say "I can take one small step."

Instead of "I must be perfect"
you can say "I can be human."

Instead of "I don't have time to relax"
say "I must take time to relax."

By not taking time for fun and relaxation, it makes us procrastinate even more. The best idea I got from Fiore's book was to set up several rewards for getting work done. Not just one big reward after all the work is done, but lots of little ones or big ones after a portion of the work is done.

For mortgage brokers, we can do seminars to attract clients. You might be afraid of this sort of marketing, but still want to do it. Well, after you schedule the seminar, take a break. After you write your speech, eat a couple of cookies. After you advertise the seminar, get a massage. This is just a simple example from the top of my head, but the theory works. Yes, it does take longer than just putting your nose to the grindstone and knocking out everything all at once. If you can do that, good for you. But try to do that 30–40 times and you'll get burned out.

So the best way to overcome procrastination is to:

- understand why you procrastinate.

- change your thinking about how to overcome it.

- change your words and speech to put yourself back in control.

- take time to enjoy life and not work yourself to death.

- give yourself multiple rewards for accomplishing small parts of your task.

- make the task as fun as possible.

THE BUSINESS PLAN

Surely you want to succeed as a loan officer. But you realize that mortgage lending is tough. You need thick skin, a hard spine, and a spirit that gives yourself every advantage possible.

In this chapter I am going to show you how to have a thought-out, customized plan for success. Writing a business plan can take you to the next level, especially since 90% of your competition doesn't have such a strategy.

Without a business plan, you will stay small. Without thinking big, you will have no motivation, no necessity to improve. Sure, as a new loan officer you have big dreams and visions. But unless you put these on paper and have a plan to accomplish them you will get caught in a day-to-day treadmill going nowhere. You want to move up by writing a business plan—an "on the business" activity. You want to review it and guide your company with exactly that vision.

What's so big about a business plan? It precisely defines your business, identifies your goals, and serves as your business's resume. It helps you allocate resources properly, handle unforeseen complications, and make good business decisions.

A comprehensive, thoughtful business plan is simply crucial.

It's a tool with three basic purposes:

As a planning tool, it guides you through various phases of your business. A thoughtful plan helps identify obstacles so you can avoid them and establish alternatives. Many business owners share their plans with employees to foster a broader understanding of where the business is going.

In the beginning, you might not have any employees. In this case, the business plan is your blueprint. It tells you where you want to go and how and when you will get there. It forces you to do research and thinking that you might otherwise avoid. Believe me, I know. I have started companies with business plans and without. The ones with them were definitely easier to grow and manage.

As a communication tool, it is used to attract investment capital, secure loans, convince workers to hire on, and assist in drawing strategic business partners. The development of a comprehensive plan shows whether a business has the potential to make a profit. It requires a realistic look at almost every phase of business. There's more. A plan shows you know what's going on; you are forced to solve problems and chose alternatives before launching your business.

As a management tool, the business plan helps you monitor your progress. The plan is a living document that you modify as you gain knowledge and experience. By using your plan to establish timelines and milestones, you can gauge your progress and compare your projections to results.

Despite the importance of a business plan, many small business owners procrastinate. They figure their marketplace changes too fast for a business plan to be useful. Or they don't want to take the time. It is a challenge for many business owners to put their assumptions on paper and risk the fact they may be wrong.

If more businesses planned, their failure rate in the first five years would drop significantly. Research shows that companies with just the strategic section of a business plan have 50% more profits and revenue than non-planning businesses.

Another survey shows companies that plan have 63% higher revenue growth and 100% more profits. Still not convinced? Consider the following reasons for business failure:

- Poor management systems.

- No overall vision.

- Lack of market planning.

- Not understanding the competition.

- No strategic plan.

- No established performance measures.

- Inadequate financial planning.

Just as a builder needs a blueprint to begin construction, eager business owners need a plan to enter new ventures. Spend at least as much time on business planning as you do on vacation planning, and you will put your business on track to success.

TYPES OF BUSINESS PLANS

Business plans are also called strategic plans, investment plans, expansion plans, operational plans, annual plans, internal plans, growth plans, product plans, and feasibility plans. These are all business plans.

A plan matches your specific situation. If you're developing a plan for internal use only, not for sending out to banks or investors, you may not need to include every background detail. Description of the management team is crucial for investors. Financial history is most important for banks.

The most standard business plan is a **startup plan.** By definition, it lays out the steps for a new business. It covers standard topics: the company, product or service, market, forecasts, strategy, implementation milestones, management team, and financial analysis. That analysis includes projected sales, profit and loss, balance sheet, and cash flow.

Internal plans are not intended for outside investors, banks, or other third parties. They might not include detailed descriptions of the company or management team. They might include detailed financial projections. The main points may appear as bullet points rather than detailed texts.

An **operations plan** is normally an internal plan, and it might also be called an internal or annual plan. It details specific implementation milestones, dates, deadlines, and responsibilities of teams and managers.

A **strategic plan** is usually also an internal plan, but it focuses more on high-level options and priorities than on detailed dates and responsibilities. Like most internal plans, it wouldn't include descriptions of the company or the management team. It might also leave out some financial projections, with points appearing as bullets in slides.

A **growth, expansion, or new product plan** will sometimes focus on a specific area of business or a subset of the business. Each plan could be internal, depending on whether it is linked to loan applications or new investments. For example, an expansion plan requiring a new investment would include full company descriptions and background on the management team, much as a startup plan for investors. Loan applications require this much detail as well. An internal plan—to set the steps for growth—might skip these descriptions. It might not include detailed financial projections for the company, but it should include forecasts of sales and expenses for the firm.

A **feasibility plan** is for startups. It includes a summary, mission statement, keys to success, basic market analysis, and preliminary analysis of costs, pricing, and probable expenses. This plan helps decide whether a business opportunity is worth pursuing.

I recommend you to do at least a feasibility plan of your opportunity as a loan officer.

SWOT Analysis

"We are great at everything and have no competitors."

Any business that thinks this way is in trouble. Focus and

realism must be applied to business planning to ensure success. One of the best exercises for getting focused and real is a SWOT analysis. You should perform one before preparing your business plan.

SWOT stands for strengths, weaknesses, opportunities, and threats. Strengths and weaknesses make your business look internally at what your company can do. Threats and opportunities push your company to be aware of the external environment. A SWOT analysis challenges you to see beyond your company to determine what opportunities exist and how to capitalize on your strengths.

Most of your analysis will be subjective, so the SWOT can benefit your small business. Benefits include:

- Insight into where your business can focus to grow.

- Understanding the industry structure by using a SWOT in your business plan.

- Focusing your advertising and marketing on areas that give you a competitive advantage.

- The ability to see and react to threats.

To develop your own SWOT analysis, consider each section realistically and be specific. To effectively complete a SWOT for your organization, consider the following examples:

Strengths

Consider your strengths relative to your competitors and from your customers' perspective. Take your competitors' way of selling vs. yours. They may use the phone. You may go the face-to-face route. If a customer wants something that you provide and your competitor doesn't, you have an advantage in the strength department.

Weaknesses

Let's face it. It's easier writing down your corporate strengths than weaknesses. This helps: Think of objections your customers raise during the sales process.

Do you feel you address these objections adequately or do you lack something your customers want?

Opportunities

All organizations can gain from opportunities. The key is finding hidden ones.

Threats

All organizations face threats. These could be internal, such as falling productivity. They could be external, such as competitors' lower fees. Consider what can make your business obsolete, and what will replace it.

The SWOT analysis is a quick and simple tool to see the big picture. It is the starting point of strategic planning. Once you have a SWOT complete, you may want to try more advanced analyses.

It's crucial to apply this knowledge to your business plan. Plan actions to reduce threats and weaknesses in your company and position yourself to take advantage of opportunities and strengths.

WRITING THE PLAN

How long should you make a business plan? Figure on 5 to 100 pages, depending on its use and audience. A basic plan for a bank usually runs 20-plus pages, including financials. An effective plan for a small business might go 5 to 10 pages, highlighting the business and direction.

Before you begin writing your plan, consider four core questions:

- What services does your business provide and what needs does it fill?

- Who are the potential customers for your product or service and why will they purchase it from you?

- How will you reach your potential customers?

- Where will you get the financial resources to start your business?

Although no single formula exists for developing a business plan, all plans share some elements. Generally, a plan includes four sections:

1) Description of the business

2) Marketing

3) Finances

4) Management

This outline can serve as a guide for your plan:

I. Executive Summary

II. The Business
   A. Description of the business
   B. Marketing
   C. Competition
   D. Operating procedures

III. Financial Data
   A. Capital equipment and supply list
   B. Balance sheet
   C. Break-even analysis

D. Income projections (profit & loss statements)
    Three-year summary
    Detail by month, first year
    Assumptions upon which projections were
    based

IV. Supporting Documents

EXECUTIVE SUMMARY

The Executive Summary is your entire plan condensed
into a page or two. When you show your plan to others, this is
the part most of them will read. So make sure it's as clear, concise, and exciting as possible. I suggest you do this part last.
After finishing the other sections, you will have an overview
of the business and can solidify it here.

DESCRIPTION OF THE BUSINESS

This section is an in-depth look at your enterprise: what
you do, your niche(s), who your customers are, what products
you sell, your operating structure, legal details of your company, and your USP. This is the section where you underscore
what makes you different in your market. What makes you
stand out? Why are you in the business and what do you add
to make it better?

If you are a seasoned pro, you can talk about where you
have been and what you have learned from those experiences.

You can also mention the things you will NOT do such as: You will not work weekends, you will not work at 7 p.m., and you will not work with overly demanding realtors.

MARKETING

This is your marketing plan. This where you go into detail regarding who your target market is, how large it is, and how you will reach it. If you are concentrating on a city or town, you should include demographic and census information. How many people are moving in, moving out, where do they work, and what percentage have kids? You can get most of that on the Internet, TV and in your newspaper.

You also need to determine what marketing tactics are best to reach your target market. This is NOT a place to list all the techniques you know. Evaluate them all and pick the top three or four that you will focus on.

List your advertising budget and see how you can afford your chosen marketing techniques. In the beginning your budget will dictate your marketing. As you experience success, put more money into the marketing that works and stop the marketing that doesn't.

This is the type of thinking, planning, and legwork you need to be successful. This is also the work that 99% of loan officers avoid and why our industry has such high turnover.

Doing what everyone else is doing only leads to burnout and misery. Plan your business the way you want it, and work to make your plan a reality.

COMPETITION

This is where you explain in detail the strengths and weaknesses of your competition. This lets you determine where to position yourself in the market in relation to your competition.

This is also the part where most loan officers feel hopeless thinking about all the other loan companies, banks, and lenders in the market. And that is why I urge you to niche yourself. The more you niche, the less competition you have. And the easier it is to get loans.

By trying to be a lender to everyone, you must compete with every other lender. By focusing on your niche, or target market, you can become the lender of choice for that niche.

Just make sure to watch the big guns. Watch their marketing and promotions. Identify their weaknesses and be ready to capitalize on them. When a company advertises flat-fee or no-fee loans, tell your clients that the only way that firm can do that is by charging a higher rate.

As an individual loan officer, you can't compare your production to behemoth loan companies like Countrywide and Quicken Loans. So compare how well you are doing to other loan officers in your office. Gauge your progress against theirs.

OPERATING PROCEDURES/DEVELOPMENT PLAN

This is where you plan to profit! Operating procedures are your rules of operation. What time are you in the office every day? What time do you knock off? How do you handle each loan? How do you handle referrals? What procedures do you use to make sure your clients experience Amazing Service™ from you and your company?

FINANCIALS

Even if you are bad at math, you'll find a big plus in this section. This is where you add up your future. Here is where you identify how much you will spend and how much you need to make. If you are losing money, how will you make up the shortfall?

Don't worry about capital requirements, balance sheets, or most of the other detailed financial statements.

Create a table of projected milestones. Estimate the month and year of the important milestones you will achieve over the next year, two years, five years. These are your goals.

The easiest way is to focus on monthly income and expenses. Start by doing a simple 12-month, cash-flow forecast.

Step 1: Estimate how much in revenue you will generate on a monthly basis. Include your loan commissions and any salary.

Step 2: Determine your monthly expenses. Itemize everything: advertising, office supplies, phone bills, subscriptions, desk fees.

Step 3: Subtract the total in Step 2 from the total in Step 1 to get your monthly Net Cash Flow. If your Net is negative, you are losing money!

It is crucial to be as honest as possible when doing these numbers. Exaggerating will only hurt you. If you forecast too much income and start spending in advance, you could be in a whole heap of trouble if those loans don't come in.

PITFALLS TO AVOID

Common errors made by first-time business plan writers include:

Putting it off.

Too many businesses make business plans only when they have no choice. Unless a bank or investors want a plan, no plan surfaces. Don't wait to write your plan until you think you'll have enough time. The busier you are, the more you need to plan. If you are always putting out fires, you should build firebreaks or a sprinkler system. You can lose the forest for paying too much attention to the burning trees.

Cash flow casualness.

Most people think in terms of profits instead of cash. When you imagine a new business, you think of what it would cost to make the product, what you could sell it for, and what the profits per unit might be. We are trained to think of business as sales minus costs and expenses, which equals profits. Unfortunately, we don't spend the profits in a business. We spend cash. So understanding cash flow is critical. If you have only one table in your business plan, make it the cash flow table.

Idea inflation.

Don't overestimate the importance of the idea. You don't need a great idea to start a business; you need time, money, perseverance, and common sense. Few successful businesses are based entirely on new ideas. A new idea is harder to sell than an existing one, because people don't understand a new idea and they are often unsure if it will work.

Being a loan officer isn't a radical thing. They have been around for a long time and will be around for a much longer time. Most of what you will come up with in terms of marketing, services, and creativity has already been done by someone else.

Fear and dread.

Doing a business plan isn't as hard as you might think. You don't have to write a doctoral thesis or a novel. There are good books to help, many advisers among the Small Business Development Centers (SBDCs), business schools, and software (such as Business Plan Pro).

Spongy, vague goals.

Leave out the vague and meaningless babble of business phrases (such as "being the best") because they are simply hype. Remember that the objective of a plan is its results, and for results you need tracking and follow-up. You need specific dates, management responsibilities, budgets, and milestones. Then you can follow up. No matter how well thought out or brilliantly presented, it means nothing unless it produces results.

One size fits all.

Tailor your plan to its real business purpose. Business plans vary. They can be detailed action plans, financial plans, marketing plans, and even personnel plans. They can be used to start a business or just run a business better.

Diluted priorities.

Remember, strategy is focus. A priority list with 3 or 4 items is focus. A priority list with 20 items is certainly not strategic, and rarely effective. The more items on the list, the less the importance of each.

Ignoring the competition.

A business does not operate in a vacuum. Direct and indirect competitors will fight hard to retain their customer base and market share. Ignoring them doesn't make them go away; it makes your business vulnerable.

One billion consumers.

Overestimating your market size paves the way for unrealistic financial projections. Focus on one or two niches you can effectively serve.

AUTOMATING BUSINESS PLAN PREPARATION

Business plan software can help you organize your plan and guide you through the process. Many excellent software products are on the market. If you use one, base your selection on the following:

Ease of use. With limited time, a busy business owner needs software easy to set up and use.

Industry Templates. The business plan software should offer templates for your business and let you edit these features for a customized look.

System Requirements. The software version available should be compatible with your computer system.

Data Input. If you are using a financial program, can you directly input your data into the business plan program? The answer better be yes.

Support. Determine the level of support available for problems or questions you may have when using the business plan software.

Collaboration. Does the business plan software have collaborative abilities if you have multiple team members or outside consultants work on the plan? You want a yes answer.

BUSINESS PLAN MONITORING

Once you have the plan written, maintain it as a living document that reflects your objectives and goals. A strategy for this is business plan monitoring, or BPM.

BPM begins with identifying performance metrics—key ratios and numbers vital to the company's success. Examples of metrics include sales conversion, lead generation, and closings. By regularly monitoring the performance metrics, you can correct problems, capitalize on opportunities, and keep the business plan current.

You might assume a 10% close rate on all qualified leads you generate. This assumption was the basis of the revenue targets in the financial section of your plan. After three months of operation, you see that you are only at a 7% close rate. This will affect your financial forecasts for the year. Knowing this, you can go back to your marketing and sales strategy to pinpoint what is going wrong. This simple metric has alerted you to a problem or to changes in the market that will let you make revisions in your operations to make the year-end forecast.

Overall, a well written and researched business plan will prepare your company for today's conditions—plus tomorrow's unforeseen events. All business plans should have a contingency section to accommodate for the future. The BPM process lets your plan become an organic business plan that will be updated when new market conditions or strategic changes take place. Review your plan periodically—at least quarterly and preferably monthly—to check the status of your metrics and make adjustments.

BUSINESS PLAN RESOURCES

Here are solid sources for more help.

The United States Small Business Administration offers excellent help for all small business owners: *http://www.sba.gov/ starting_business/planning/basic.html*

The Yahoo Small Business Center has information about business plans: *http://smallbusiness.yahoo.com/resources/business_ plans.html*

The Annual Moot Corp Competition challenges MBAs from around the world to submit their plans to be evaluated by investors. You can view a few of the past winning entries: *http://www.BusinessPlans.org/MootCorp.html*

Canada Business Service Centers has an interactive planner that leads you through creating a three-year business plan: *http://www.cbsc.org/ibp*

Besides the Internet, your library and bookstore are packed with information on business plans.

After you have written your plan, use it as a guide of your business. If you do it properly, you will constantly go back to it for information. It will help you in your current situation and measure how well you achieved your goals.

Your plan should not be a one-time thing. Keep updating it. After a while you will see where you were, where you are going and the best way to get there.

CHAPTER 7

WHY ARE WE DOING THIS?

Are you meandering through life or on a serious mission? Do you have a vision for your life's direction? Is your action driven by your outlook or your values?

Make those visions and values come alive. How? Create a personal mission statement like the one introduced in Stephen Covey's *The Seven Habits of Highly Effective People*.

A large percentage of companies, including most of the Fortune 500, have corporate mission statements. Such statements are designed to provide direction and thrust. They give an organization an enduring statement of purpose. A mission statement acts as an invisible hand that guides the people in the organization. A mission statement explains the organization's reason for being and answers the question, "What business are we in?"

In his book *First Things First,* Covey points out that mission statements are often not taken seriously in organizations because they are developed by top executives. Thus there's no buy-in at the lower levels. You can bet there's buy-in when we develop our own mission statements.

A personal mission statement differs from a company mission statement, but the principles are the same. Writing a personal mission statement lets you establish what's important personally and professionally. It also lets you chart a new course when you're at a career intersection. Covey refers to a personal mission statement as "connecting with your own unique purpose and the profound satisfaction that comes from fulfilling it."

WHY A PERSONAL MISSION STATEMENT?

In this book, we focus more on the individual loan officer and not the mortgage brokerage business. So welcome to the personal mission statement, not corporate mission statement.

Your business/company is an extension of you. As you grow and perhaps open your own company, you should use your personal mission statement to help create your corporate one.

Remember, being a loan officer is still just a job. It does not define who you are as a person. And your job should not run your life. Unfortunately, most loan officers don't understand this concept. Of course money is crucial, but more important things exist. A personal mission statement can put your career in perspective with the rest of your life.

THE KEY BENEFITS OF A PERSONAL MISSION STATEMENT

Developing a personal mission statement can help you focus on what you want to be (your character), what you want to do (contribution and achievements) and what you want to have in life.

A personal mission statement is a personal constitution. Like the United States Constitution, it's fundamentally changeless. A personal mission statement based on correct principles sets the standard for an individual. It becomes the basis for making life-directing decisions. It empowers people with timeless strength amid change.

With a mission statement, you can flow while everything changes around you. The key is knowing what you value. You don't need prejudgments or prejudices. You don't need to stereotype and categorize everything and everybody in order to accommodate reality.

Your personal environment changes constantly. Rapid change burns out many people. They become reactive and essentially give up.

Once you have a sense of mission, you have the vision and understand the values that direct your life. You have the basic direction from which you can set your long- and short-term goals. You have the power of a written constitution based on correct principles, against which every decision concerning the most effective use of your time, talent and energy can be measured.

A personal mission statement:

- Gives meaning to your actions.

- Provides focus to all of your roles (parent, employee, friend, spouse, etc.).

- Eliminates confusion and emotional conflicts.

- Is the best tool to measure any large life choices.

- Helps eliminate unproductive activities.

- Puts first things first.

- Lets you clearly tell others what you can do for them.

- Keeps circumstances from distracting you.

- Tells you to use all of your skills.

- Requires that you use skills for the benefit of others.

- Provides a rock of stability.

- Provides a forward direction that brings peace and integrity to changing times.

- Keeps you from letting others take the steering wheel of your life.

- Helps you choose the best course of action.

- Sets you up to know that the more you live your mission, the more those around you will respect and support your actions.

Charting Your Professional (and Personal) Course

OK, a personal mission statement is valuable. So how do you go about crafting one? That's the biggest challenge.

One way is to begin with the end in mind. When you have a picture of where you would like to end up, you can better see where you are and what steps you need to take to bridge the gap.

Visualize your 80th birthday or 50th wedding anniversary and imagine what all your friends and family would say about you (a more morbid approach is writing your own obituary). Record everything you "hear" people say in your visualization, and use this as the foundation for the statement.

Brainstorm with yourself, family members, teachers, religious leaders, counselors, and friends about your strengths, talent, deep-felt values and principles that are most important to you. Read biographies of heroes to identify traits that you admire and principles you adhere to. Take personality/ aptitude/vocational tests to pinpoint talent and skills.

You want to build your mission statement on a foundation of correct principles. Unlike other centers based on people and things subject to frequent change (e.g., money, pleasure, even your spouse), correct principles don't change. We can depend on them. We are drawn away from effectiveness when we make our center something other than our principles.

Now that you have this information, find a quiet place so you can ponder and write your personal mission statement. Keep it short—no more than a page or a few paragraphs.

It doesn't have to totally reflect where you are today. It should help you stretch to improve and serve as a guide when you need to make difficult decisions. Write in the present tense, as if you are already doing it. It should inspire you and cause you to stretch, but not break.

Take a break—an hour, a day, a week. Then come back to what you have written and ask yourself, "Does this statement inspire me?" If the answer is "no" or "maybe," spend more time crafting it until you can answer a definite "yes."

Your mission statement may take you weeks to write, from first draft to final form; it's a concise expression of your innermost values and directions. After finishing, you will want to review it regularly and make minor changes as the years bring new insights

A PERSONAL MISSION STATEMENT RECIPE

If you hit a roadblock in creating your mission statement, don't be discouraged. Take a deep breath, relax, and brainstorm for 10 or 15 minutes.

Take out a blank sheet of paper or bring up a blank document on your computer. Ask yourself: What are you personally looking for, yearning for, hoping for? What are your passions? Why are you in business for yourself? Chances are you would not start something you did not enjoy, because your success would be limited from the beginning.

Don't think; just write. Don't worry about making sense; just let the words flow. One word, phrase or sentence at a time. This will help unblock your mind as well as remind you what your project is all about.

If the writing process is still tough, here is a step-by-step approach to crafting a statement that is powerful and authentic. Take as much time on each step as you need—and remember to dig deeply to develop a mission statement that is authentic and honest.

Identify past successes.

Find four or five examples of personal success in recent years—at work, in your community, at home. Write them down. Try to identify a common theme through these examples. Write it down.

Identify core principles.

List attributes that identify who you are and what your priorities are. Then see if you can narrow your values down to five or six crucial ones. Finally, choose the one value most important to you.

Identify contributions.

List ways you could make a difference. In an ideal situation, how could you contribute best to:

- the world in general

- your family

- your employer or future employers

- your friends

- your community

Identify goals.

Spend time thinking about your priorities and goals. List your personal goals in the short term (up to three years) and the long term (beyond three years).

Write your personal mission statement.

Based on the first four steps and a better understanding of yourself, begin writing your personal mission statement.

An example of this process may help you. Here is how a person in a different professional field might approach it:

Past successes:

- Developed new features for stagnant product.

- Part of team that developed new positioning statement for product.

- Helped child's school with fundraiser that was wildly successful.

- Increased turnout for the opening of a new local theater company.

Themes: Successes all relate to creative problem solving and execution of a solution.

Core values:

- Hard-working

- Industrious

- Creative

- Problem solver

- Decision maker

- Friendly

- Outgoing

- Positive

- Family-oriented

- Honest

- Intelligent

- Compassionate

- Spiritual

- Analytical

- Passionate

- Contemplative

Most important values:

- Problem solver

- Creative

- Analytical

- Compassionate

- Decision maker

- Positive

Most important value:

- Creative

Contributions:

- The world in general: develop products and services that help people achieve what they want in life; have a lasting impact on the way people live.

- My family: be a leader in terms of personal outlook, compassion for others, and maintaining an ethical code; be a good mother and a loving wife; leave the world a better place for my children and their children.

- My employer or future employers: lead by example and demonstrate how innovative and problem-solving products can be successful in terms of solving a problem and in terms of profitability and revenue generation for the organization.

- My friends: always have a hand held out for my friends; for them to know they can always come to me with any problem.

- My community: use my talents to give back to my community.

Goals:

- Short term: continue my career with a progressive employer that lets me use my skills, talent, and values to achieve success for the firm.

- Long term: develop other outlets for my talent and develop a longer-term plan for diversifying my life and achieving professional and personal success.

Mission Statement:

To live life completely, honestly, and compassionately, with a healthy dose of realism mixed with the imagination and dreams that all things are possible if one sets her mind to finding an answer.

MORE EXAMPLES

Because each individual is unique, a personal mission statement will reflect that uniqueness, both in content and form.

Here is how one person articulated his statement:

- Succeed at home first.

- Seek and merit divine help.

- Never compromise with honesty.

- Remember the people involved.

- Hear both sides before judging.

- Obtain counsel of others.

- Defend those who are absent.

- Be sincere, yet decisive.

- Develop one new proficiency a year.

- Plan tomorrow's work today.

- Hustle while you wait.

- Maintain a positive attitude.

- Keep a sense of humor.

- Be orderly in person and in work.

- Do not fear mistakes; fear only the absence of creative, constructive, and corrective responses to those mistakes.

- Facilitate the success of subordinates.

- Listen twice as much as you speak.

- Concentrate all abilities and efforts on the task at hand, not worrying about the next job or promotion.

A woman seeking to balance family and work values may express her sense of personal mission differently:

- I will seek to balance career and family as best I can, since both are important to me.

- My home will be a place where I and my family, friends, and guests find joy, comfort, peace, and happiness. I will seek to create a clean and orderly environment. I will exercise wisdom in what we choose to eat, read, see, and do at home. I especially want to teach my children to love, learn, and laugh—plus work and develop their unique talents.

- I value the rights, freedoms, and responsibilities of our democratic society. I will be a concerned and informed citizen, involved in the political process to ensure my voice is heard and my vote is counted.

- I will be a self-starting individual who exercises initiative in accomplishing my life's goals. I will act on situations and opportunities, rather than be acted upon.

- I will always try to keep myself free from addictive and destructive habits. I will develop habits that free me from old labels and limits and expand my capabilities and choices.

- My money will be my servant, not my master. I will seek financial independence over time. My wants will be subject to my needs and my means. Except for long-term home and car loans, I will seek to keep myself free from consumer debt. I will spend less than I earn and regularly save or invest part of my income.

- I will use what money and talents I have to make life more enjoyable for others through service and charitable giving.

FINAL THOUGHTS

A personal mission statement is *personal*. But if you want to truly see whether you have been honest in developing your personal mission statement, consider sharing the results of this process with close friends. Ask for their feedback.

Finally, remember that a mission statement is not meant to be written once and then carved into stone. While fundamentally timeless, your mission statement needs to be periodically reviewed as you grow and change. Set aside time annually to review your statement and make adjustments. Questions to ask include:

- Is my mission based on timeless principles? What are they?

- Does it represent the best within me?

- Do I feel good about what this mission statement represents?

- Do I feel direction, purpose, challenge, and motivation when I read it?

- What skills and strategies will help me live up to the goals I've set within my mission?

- Does my mission statement inspire me?

Use these and other questions to prompt you to modify your statement so it evolves with you as you proceed through life. This way, you will continue to benefit from one of the most powerful tools in your success toolbox.

CHAPTER 8

WORKING ON THE BUSINESS

Work on your business instead of in it.

Interesting concept, no? But what does it mean?

People in our industry tend to jump headfirst into the business. And that is great. But they jump in without checking how deep the water is. That can hurt. So can going from one loan to another, never seeing their business for what it is—a business.

Working 60–70 hours a week, driving around town every day, and catering to realtors, builders, title companies, and borrowers is no way to run a business. Putting out fires all day long is not your job. Your No. 1 responsibility is to make sure you have enough leads in your pipeline. And how do you do that?

By working on the business instead of in it.

Here are some examples:

Working on the business	Working in the business
Creating a new marketing campaign	Delivering loan docs to the lender
Analyzing your marketing effectiveness	Calling borrowers to get more info for conditions
Setting goals for growth	Inputting 1003 info into your loan software
Educating yourself	Dealing with the listing agent wanting an update
Crafting your own USP	Ordering an appraisal
Tracking your marketing	Paying the bills
Analyzing your conversion rates	Driving to a prospect's house to sell him a loan
Learning objection handling techniques	Answering emails from prospects

In a nutshell: Working on your business is everything you do to grow the business, streamline it, and make it easier to run and manage. Working in the business is everything that needs to be done on a daily basis to keep things going.

Why is this important?

The best way to grow your business and your income is to work on it. You want to get to the point where the business does not need you.

What would happen to your business if you could not work one or more months?

That's realistic. You can get sick, or suffer an accident. The result can be disastrous. I have met many people who lost everything because of an illness to themselves or a loved one. It's horrible to think about.

But you must think about it. What shape would your business be in if you left it for a month?

I ask that to our new coaching members, and many times they answer, "A whole month? I don't need that long. I'd be out of business in two weeks if I weren't there."

The great thing about our profession is we don't have jobs and set hours, so if you have enough money in the bank you could last a month without income, and pick up where you left off. But you would still have to come back when the money ran out.

What we want to do is create a business that runs without us—all the time. Sure, you'd have to check up on it, but you wouldn't have to put in the hours and deal with daily frustrations.

This works for an individual loan officer as well as the broker who wants to have the largest mortgage company in the country.

By working on your business, you can create your dream life. Here is a story of a person who worked on his business, and how things turned out.

THE LONG-DISTANCE RUNNER

This man owns a company. And has dozens of loan officers working for him. His company is setting growth records that will make it the largest mortgage brokerage in the state in the next two years.

He rises early (he loves seeing the sunrise) each morning and jogs two miles with his wife before they wake the kids and she drops them at their private school while he heads for work.

He is usually home by 5 p.m., spends weekends with the family, lives in the nicest part of town, and drives a new car every three years. (He has a thing for European sports cars.) The three months of vacation every year are nice, too.

He still services his database of personal clients and takes their applications himself, mainly because he loves people. The same clients have been coming back to him again and again through the years; they are more like friends than clients. He doesn't have time to handle the dozens of new clients referred to him every week, so he has his other loan officers handle that duty.

It's no surprise he loves his life. He is downright proud he has made all his dreams come true. He has a business that will make him money, whether he is there or not. He enjoys his work because he works with people who want to work with him, and his clients trust him completely.

Sounds great, doesn't it? It can be great for you too if you implement the strategies outlined in this course.

THE GOLDEN ARCHES

How many McDonald's have you eaten at? Maybe dozens. And at each one you have probably noticed the same décor, uniforms, even food. I know I can walk into any McDonald's today, order a cheeseburger and get the same taste as the last one I ordered and the one before that. That's what I've come to expect. And that's exactly what Ray Kroc envisioned when he started McDonald's back in 1952.

He wanted to create a business that would work, no matter who was working it. He developed a system-dependent business rather than a people-dependent business. His business could be bought by anyone and produce the same quality as another one 10,000 miles away run by someone else.

How did he do it? He simply built his business as a franchise prototype. He produced a company that works this way: A system runs the business, and people run the system.

You're probably thinking, "But my business is no McDonald's." Maybe not. But wouldn't it be nice if your business could survive without you a few days and still produce the quality your customers have come to expect when you're there? All you have to do is pretend your business is a prototype and that you want to have more just like it—exactly like it.

Surveys show that over 70% of all new loan officers quit within their first year. And that 40% of seasoned loan officers quit every year. That's a huge amount of turnover. The purpose here is to help you beat the odds and succeed.

You can help yourself by implementing a proper system. The secret? Work on your business.

The five biggest reasons people fail:

1. They don't do anything. If you don't try, you can't succeed.

2. They do everything halfway. Ideas are great, but if you start too many things and never follow through, you will not achieve maximum rewards.

3. They aren't consistent. You must have a system. You can't leave out a step and expect everything to work.

4. They have no plan. Without one, you can't know where to begin and what to do next.

5. They procrastinate. Don't make excuses. If you're waiting for everything to be perfect before you start, you never will because things will never be perfect.

THE STAGES OF YOUR BUSINESS

What stage is your business in right now?

Infancy: You and your business are one. You're consumed. You eat, sleep, and breathe mortgages. Be careful. You cannot continue at this pace for too long. Eventually you won't be able to handle everything. All the enthusiasm will begin to fade; you will start resenting this business and everything associated with it.

Adolescence: You realize you cannot do everything by yourself. Maybe you're thinking of bringing in outside help. Don't let this new-found freedom give you false security. It is still up to you to bring in the loans.

Maturity: Your business has grown, has a well-defined future, and you know how to take it to the next level.

Chances are you are in Infancy or Adolescence. And it is great that you are advancing toward maturity. Remember, you need to keep motivating yourself as your business grows. You will find ups and downs along the way. Probably a lot of them.

The best way to limit the downs is to set up a proper system. If you want your business to grow, you must work on it.

The book that really introduced us to the "work on the business concept" was *The E-Myth Revisited* by Michael Gerber. I highly recommend it. Gerber breaks down what he terms the "entrepreneurial myth," assuring readers that we do not have to be geniuses to be successful in our businesses. He stresses that entrepreneurs have to work smart.

Gerber explains that three people exist inside each individual: the technician, the manager, and the entrepreneur. The technician lives for the present, the manager in the past, and the entrepreneur in the future. It's necessary to have all three personalities, but they must be properly balanced for you to achieve success.

Most loan officers are so busy being technicians, they have no time to work on their business. As they get busier, they hire assistants to help them accomplish all the tasks. At that point, they must be a manager as well.

That's when the business has an "entrepreneurial seizure," as Gerber calls it. The technician is juggling the technician and manager roles, so service and production dive. Sales slip, and the loan officer blames the new assistant. The assistant is fired or relegated to menial tasks and starts to resent the loan officer.

This is so common that many loan officers are afraid to hire assistants. While it is crucial to pick the right person for the job, having a proper system in place makes sure the transition is smoother and easier for the business.

In order to avoid a seizure, the entrepreneur must figure out a better way of doing business. We have to get beyond the technician and manager roles. We have to take the time to work on the business. We need to develop a system from the lowest levels of operations on up, so that our system works and business continues regardless of fluctuations in staff.

When your system is good, your staff becomes good. And when a staff member takes an extended leave or you add new members, a good system makes sure replacements and new hires keep the operation humming.

Take time to work on your system. Make it as efficient as a Swiss watch. In a perfect business, you would work only on things that create massive leverage for yourself. Everything else would be handled by your system.

THE RAINMAKER THEORY

You are the Rainmaker. You should only do things that you can affect. If you cannot change the outcome, have someone else do it. Here are examples of Rainmaker activities:

- Taking applications.

- Returning calls.

- Working on your business.

- Training your team.

- Public appearances.

- Keeping in touch with past clients.

- Working on your marketing.

- Watching your office run (thinking).

You should not be:

- Answering your own phone.

- Processing paperwork.

- Preparing mail-outs.

- Going to the post office.

- Doing anything else that can be done by someone who makes less per hour than you do.

Of course, if you are struggling for business, you cannot go out and hire people right away. But as you implement the strategies in this book, business will grow and you will have to hire people. Already having a system in place will make it 1,000 times easier.

Do This One Thing for Enormous Profit

As we discussed in the Time Management chapter of this book, you should have a daily schedule. You should set aside time each day to work on your business. If you do nothing else, this one technique will bring you tremendous wealth:

Do one thing each day that can bring in new business.

If you do not want to do anything else, this one activity will lead to a lot of business. Each day do something. Just one thing. If you do more, that's great. But even if you are so busy you don't have time to eat, you still must do at least one.

- It could be writing a postcard for a mailing.

- Or calling a past client to ask for a referral.

- Or sending an email to your email list of prospects.

- Or adding a headline to your business card.

- Or meeting with a realtor/builder/CPA for lunch.

- Or anything else that can result in more leads and loans.

What you do does not matter, as long as it brings in business. One thing each day equals 20 for the month. That is powerful stuff. Out of 20, if only one brings in a loan that month, that's worth it.

Most loan officers do not market on a daily basis. Nor do they improve their businesses on a daily basis. That is why they do not grow. They are victims of the market. If the market is booming and rates are low, they do well. If times are tough, they starve. You will not. By doing this one simple act daily, you insure yourself against failure.

SECTION 2
KNOW YOUR NUMBERS

O k. Your business has been designed, your foundation is set, and you know where you and your business are headed. Now it is time to learn how to get it there.

Knowing Your Numbers is a crucial step in the process. I would say that not performing this step is one of the largest mistakes all loan officers make. Your numbers are the key to a profitable, reliable business.

If you want a business that works for you, instead of the other way around, then you must know your numbers. I have seen too many new loan officers work their tails off to make less than they used to make in their jobs working 9–5. But once they understand that this is a business and must be treated as such, their income levels take off.

Think about it, does the CEO of any Fortune 500 company do the work himself? Nope. His job is to know the numbers and make sure the company is headed in the right direction. At any time, he can gauge how the company is doing, just by looking at the numbers.

And you will be able to do the same. The numbers you will learn about and start to track will show you what areas of your business you need to work on and improve. They will show you if you are on track to achieve your goals or not. They will keep you accountable and provide the motivation to keep you from slacking off.

Numbers don't lie.

By knowing yours, you are one step closer to an automatic business that can run without you.

CHAPTER 9

WHAT TO TRACK

In this chapter we are going to identify the different areas of your business you need to keep track of from a marketing point of view. Here are the major categories we will be working with:

Major Goals Categories:
- **Leads**
- **Cost Per Lead**
- **Interviews**
- **Applications**
- **Closings**
- **Cost Per Closing**
- **Average Commission**
- **Database**

- **Referrals**
- **Referral Partners**

You need to create goals (at least monthly, more frequently if you are doing enough volume) for each of these categories. Every category listed above is crucial to your success as a loan officer. By focusing on these numbers and on increasing your performance, you can automatically improve your business.

Leads—Based on your conversion rates, how many leads do you need every month?

Once you define your goal, you can determine what different marketing concepts you want to try. Different marketing campaigns will bring in different results. Once you find one that you like, you can then refine your ads or marketing pieces to increase response.

Cost Per Lead—Based on how much you make per loan and how much you want to keep at the end of the month, how much can you spend per lead? I believe that you should not under any circumstance spend more than this number. On the other hand, you might think that breaking even on a loan is acceptable because of the TCV and the potential for referrals. Maybe so, but I still feel that you should make money on every loan. Once the application is made, then you can determine what you want to charge. But do not spend more than your allowable Cost Per Lead.

An example would be to purchase leads for $30 each. If you purchase 100, your cost would be $3,000. If out of these 100 leads you close 2 loans and earn $1,500 on each then you would break even. So your cost per lead of $30 is too much.

Interview—How many interviews with prospects do you want every month? The more the better. By having a goal and tracking the number of interviews, you can see if you are on track to hit the month's income goal.

Applications—How many applications will you take this month? Whether you take more or less than your goal, you need to figure out why. If you took more loans than your goal, why? Was there something you did differently? Or was it a fluke that will never happen again? Taking less means there is a problem somewhere in your system.

You can also view this as a ratio. What is the percentage of people who make a loan application with you out of the total interviews that you do? In other words, how many apps (loan applications) are you getting from your interviews? 10%? 20%? 50%? As you become a better salesperson, your application rate will increase.

The hardest part is getting people in the door to meet with you. The interview is the second hardest part. Here is where you convince the prospects that you are the best loan officer for the job. The better you do, the more loans you will get and the less you can spend on marketing.

Example: You are spending $1,000 a month, getting 10 interviews and getting 2 apps out of those 10 interviews. You can easily double your income with no more work if you can increase your app rate to 4 out of 10.

Become a better salesperson by being seen as the expert, offering what no one else does, being referred, knowing how to overcome objections, and bonding with the prospects.

Closings—How many closings do you need per month to reach your income goal? Without closings you are just working for free.

Not every loan app will close. But if you pre-qualify properly and have enough lenders, most should. You will also have prospects who decide not to close on the house for one reason or another. That is something we cannot control.

What will really boil your blood is when someone makes a loan app with you, and then goes to another lender if the rate is even an eighth of a point lower than yours. This could happen after you lock the loan and rates drop or if the prospect keeps shopping your rate. If you have already locked the loan, make sure to talk to your company manager or owner to see how to handle this situation. When you lock a loan and do not deliver to the lender, they can get pretty upset.

You should also keep track of what percentage of loan apps close. If you are at less than 80%, you need to seriously look at why and fix whatever is wrong.

Cost Per Closing—How much should you spend per client to generate a lead, convert the lead into a prospect, application and then close? What is the amount you can spend per loan and still stay profitable? Make sure to include all fees and expenses that you incur. And don't forget the after closing expenses such as a closing gift.

Average Commission—How much do you want to make per loan? It takes the same amount of work to do a $100,000 loan as it does to do a $1 million dollar loan. In fact, I feel that loans less than $80,000 are the costliest to do in terms of income per hour. How much do you want to make per hour? If you are not making enough, find a way to either do less work or increase the amount you make for each loan. You can do this by nicheing, by working more with referrals, by working in a nicer part of town where home prices are higher, by increasing fees, or by lowering expenses.

Database—How many people will you add to your database every month? Unless you want to prospect and focus on generating leads your entire career, you must build as large a database as you can. And the faster you do it, the better. Our research shows that the loan officers with the largest databases make more money, work fewer hours, and enjoy the business much more than those with a smaller (or no) database.

The average person knows 300 people. That should be your beginning goal: to have 300 people in your database. I cannot stress the importance of this enough. And that is why I spent so much time on how to build, classify, and maintain your database in our *Referrals on Demand* product.

Referrals—How many referrals do you want to generate each month? Yes, the number is up to you. And there are ways to manipulate how many you get. Providing Amazing Service™ and regular contact are the cornerstones. But you also must know how to ask.

Referral Partners—How many other professionals and companies do you want to be working with to generate referrals for yourself and to generate referrals to give out? By developing a group of referral partners you can extend your marketing reach without spending any money. Realtors, accountants, financial planners, insurance agents, dry cleaners, car salesmen, divorce attorneys, politicians, and home inspectors are just a few of the kinds of businesses you can tap into to generate referrals.

Just like you have goals for all the other categories, you should set a goal to add referral partners to your database as well. Meeting and networking with new people are activities that can bring you great rewards when done on a systematic and long term basis. By just adding one new referral partner a month, and then capitalizing on the partnership, can bring you multiple loans for years and years.

CHAPTER 10

CONVERSION RATES

To be successful in this business, you must treat it as a business. You should always be organized and disciplined.

The best way to advance your business is by knowing your numbers. They are the evaluators of how you are doing and the predictors of what you will do. If your numbers show you have been getting fewer leads the last few weeks, you know for sure you will be doing fewer loans in the future.

Every business needs to track their numbers. Retail stores track their numbers every day: cash flow, inventory turnover, employee retention, same store sales vs. last year, and breakage. You must do the same. If you don't, your business will bounce around from one month to the next.

The greatest complaint loan officers have is that this business is not stable. They're wrong. It is stable—if you know how to track the numbers and take action based on what they show. If you know your numbers, you can have a predictable business that runs by itself.

Have you ever desperately needed a boatload of money fast? Maybe a family member needed surgery or you wanted a nice vacation. If you know your numbers, you're in the money. Make just a few tweaks in your system, and suddenly the results and cash appear.

Know your numbers and the business gets boring. That's boredom you can seriously live with: no more guessing where your next loan is coming from and how much you will make. Numbers don't lie.

Numbers are everywhere, and you better keep track of them. The first ones to watch are money coming in vs. money going out. Others are equally important, yet most loan officers don't even know about them.

Timeout. Let's go over vocabulary so we are on the same page.

Lead: Anyone interested in a loan.

Prospect: Anyone actively looking for a mortgage company to work with.

Appointment: A meeting with a prospect.

Application: Getting the 1003 loan application filled out along with money for credit and appraisal and/or loan application fee.

Closing: When the loan closes and you get paid.

Referral: A person who comes to you and was recommended by someone else. Most referrals are good prospects that are easy to turn into appointments.

Database: The people in your sphere of influence whom you regularly communicate with and who know you.

HERE ARE KEY CONVERSION RATES:

Lead Generation Rate:

How many leads to get one prospect?

Appointment Rate:

How many prospects does it take for you to get an appointment?

Application Rate:

How many appointments does it take to get an application?

Approval Rate:

How many applications does it take for you to close a loan?

How many loans does it take per month to pay your bills?

Answer these simple questions, and you know exactly how many prospects you need each month. You do your marketing accordingly.

The average loan officer thinks the only way to get more loans is to get more prospects. But by adjusting any of these numbers, you can make more money without having to get any more prospects. To improve your conversion rate, pre-sell your prospects better. Show them that only you have the solution to their problems.

If your application rate is low, instill confidence in your prospects that you can do the job.

If your approval rate is low, you might need better lenders and a better pre-approval process. If you need too many loans to pay the bills, you are not charging enough.

Numbers don't lie. If you want more money, improve your conversion rates. Average loan officers ignore their numbers. They do not know where to improve because they do not know how they are doing in the first place.

Set up a simple tracking system. On an Excel Spreadsheet or even a piece of paper, make a system that can help you track and analyze your numbers on a daily/weekly/monthly basis.

Here is an example:

January

Date	Leads	Prospects	Appointments	Applications	Closings
Jan 1–7	75	15	8	6	0

This simple chart shows that this person got 75 leads that week and determined that 15 were actually prospects. Out of those 15, he converted eight to appointments. Out of those eight, he got six loans. And he had no closings in the week.

So his conversion rates are as follows:

- Lead Generation Rate: 15/75 = 20%

- Appointment Rate: 8/15 = 53%

- Application Rate: 6/8 = 75%

- Approval Rate: Not enough time has gone by.

Let's use the above chart and assume this loan officer later had four closings. So his Approval Rate is 66%. Let's also assume that this loan officer earns $2,000 per closing on average. So if this loan officer gets 75 leads a week, he will close four loans and earn $8,000.

In a break-even scenario, this loan officer can afford to spend $106 to acquire one lead. By using this information, we can see that this loan officer has many options when it comes to lead generation because he can afford to pay so much. This will let him use methods of marketing that other loan officers would not use. It also tells us what he can spend on leads if he were to buy them from another company. If he were paying $25 a lead, that means he will make $81 per lead he buys! If he can keep the same conversion rates, my advice is buy as many leads as he can find.

Once you know your numbers, you can determine how many leads you need daily to reach your income goals. Another example:

Let's say you want to earn $10,000 a month in commission.

You make $2,000 a loan. So you need five loans a month. And your conversion rates are as follows:

- Lead Generation Rate: 20%.

- Appointment Rate: 35%.

- Application Rate: 50%.

- Approval Rate: 80%.

So how many leads do you need to earn $10,000 a month?

Five loans divided by 80% = 6.25 applications needed— round up to seven.

Seven applications divided by 50% = 14 appointments needed.

Fourteen appointments divided by 35% = 40 prospects needed.

Forty prospects divided by 20% = 200 leads needed.

Two hundred leads divided by 20 days a month = 10 leads a day needed to earn $10,000 a month.

Can you generate 10 leads per weekday? If so, you will earn $100,000 a year and be able to take two full months off. That's a pretty good incentive!

The different rates in detail:

Lead Generation Rate: This rate depends on the nature of your marketing. If you are targeting the right crowd, this rate should be high. In marketing circles, this is called "message to market match." Say you send fliers to an apartment complex. You might get a lot of leads, but if the people who respond do not earn enough, those leads are worthless.

In order to boost your Lead Generation Rate, target your market as much as you can. Use the other strategies discussed in this book, such as niche marketing, rapport building with your sphere of influence, working with referral partners, and using your website to qualify people before you work with them.

Appointment Rate: Once you identify prospects, you must get them to meet with you or find a way to develop relationships so you can land interviews. I use the word interviews because this is the method most loan officers use to take loan applications, but you could do it via phone, fax, or your website.

This is actually the pre-sell stage—where you can shine as a loan officer. This is your first real contact with people, so make it count. WOW them. Make yourself stand out.

Some loan officers send out welcome packs. These could be anything from info about you and directions to your office to a multimedia presentation with a book, DVD, CD, and testimonials from past clients.

The welcome pack is just one way to exhibit Amazing Service™. For more on how that can launch your profits, take a look at www.ReferralsOnDemand.com.

This is the stage where you earn your pay. You must get your prospects to take the next step. Make it easy for them. Part-time loan officers and those working from home often visit a prospect at home to take the application. This house-call service has its ups and downs, but several of our customers have reported good results.

Here's another number to track: How many times must you contact a prospect in order to land an interview? Must you send follow-up material? Call him three or more times?

Let's say a person responds to an ad you placed offering free information for homebuyers. You send this person the information and later call him to confirm if he got it and if he is a prospect. Once you know he is a prospect, the next move is leading him to your office. Two questions: How long does that process take? What must you do to get him there?

Marketing studies show it takes more than five contacts to convert most people to a sale. This means you must interact with the prospect (phone, letter, postcard, meeting) at least five times before he feels comfortable enough to agree to your request. I have tried this principle in our office, and it works. We have follow-up sequences for prospects, realtors, referral partners, and even media. As soon as someone raises his hand or we identify someone we want to work with, we keep contacting him until we get our way.

The fewer contacts you need, the better. Remember to take into account the cost of contacts when determining your budgets and deciding if your marketing is cost effective.

Application Rate: Once you have the prospects in front of you, can you get them to commit? Can you convince them you are the only loan officer for the job? Can you get them to trust you, believe you, and unfold their wallets?

Later in the book we cover the psychological factors involved with converting prospects into applications, including suggestions on how to arrange your office, present yourself, present your company, understand your prospects' needs, and make them feel at ease.

Approval Rate: If you are doing everything properly, this should be your highest rate. Simply put, the majority of applications you take should close. If you are losing a lot of loans because they are not getting approved by lenders, you (a) need more and better lenders, (b) are not pre-qualifying properly, or (c) have flawed processing procedures.

If you are losing clients to other companies, you did not pre-sell properly. By building rapport with your prospects and getting them to like you, you can eliminate this problem. If the problem is they are getting a better rate elsewhere, you need to re-evaluate your pricing structure.

Many times, your prospects will go to other companies even after applying with you. Chances are the other firms will try to steal the loan. You need certain safeguards to avoid that. A loan application fee is one such safeguard. Also, during interviews you can tell your prospects to shop around before they finally decide.

That problem is rare if you are working in a niche. Prospects see you as a friend, expert, and the one on their side—like having a family member in the business.

CONVERSION AND REFERRALS

Referrals are the other major way to generate business. And working with referrals creates its own conversion rates.

The top two conversion rates for referrals are:

Database Response Rate:

How many people in your database do you need to get a referral? If you have 300 people in your database and you get three referrals a year, your Database Response Rate is 1%. That's horrible.

If you get one referral for every person in your database, you are at 100%. Work your database properly, and you can get more than one loan per person in your database.

As you classify the people in your database, you will see that some do not deserve to be there. As you cut the undesirables, your rate will increase.

Referral Application Rate:

How many referrals does it take to get an application? This is similar to the Application Rate, but still different because you can manipulate this rate. By teaching your database and referral partners how to sell you, you can increase this rate incredibly. As you increase your skills in asking for referrals, and in providing Amazing Service™, you will see your Referral Application Rate climb to almost 100%.

By concentrating on your numbers, you can tell exactly where you need to improve to increase your net profits. You can also predict how many loans you will get and how much you will make in future months, by looking at current numbers. Spend time working on each number. Figure out how you can improve your results. Set up systems that can help you convert as many leads to closing as possible.

SECTION 3

WHO WANTS A LOAN?

ere is the section you have been waiting for. Generating leads is the lifeblood of our business. It doesn't matter how many loan options you have, or how low your rates are, or how many years of experience you have. Without leads and prospects you are a starving loan officer.

This section will show you multiple ways to make sure you have enough leads to get your business humming. The following five chapters provide you the framework to put together your own marketing plan. Lead generation is an art form. But if you keep at it, and keep learning, you too can become a master.

Lead generating comes down to marketing. How good are you at marketing? Whatever your answer, you can always get better. And it is in your best interest to do so. I am going to share with you some of the basics of prospecting, dozens of cheap methods of prospecting, and a few well defined marketing ideas that have been and are generating thousands of leads for loan officers using them.

A coaching client once asked me, "Why should we bother with marketing when we can just buy leads?"

My answer is that you should have multiple ways to generate leads. You cannot become dependant on just one method. And when you do the marketing, you know the quality of the lead. Most leads that you can purchase are not high quality and are way overpriced. This is not to say that you should never buy leads. If you find a source that has good leads at a fair price then go for it. Whatever makes your life easier. But keep your own marketing running at the same time.

As a loan officer working on commission, you job is to bring in the loans. You cannot have loans if you do not have leads. So your #1 job is to generate leads. And this is the hardest part of the business. If generating leads was easy, we wouldn't get paid the big bucks. My aim in this section is to get you thinking about lead generation in new ways, and for you to learn what it takes to generate leads and how to go about doing it.

HOW MANY LEADS DO YOU WANT?

In the past, loan officers relied on real estate agents for all their business. They would try to make friends with agents and wait until they brought the buyers to them. It worked great for the loan officers: no marketing expense, no work involved. Just have buyers brought to you.

It doesn't work that way anymore. The trend across the country is for agents to become loan officers as well. Mortgage companies are opening inside the real estate offices. There are more loan officers and realtors than ever before.

If you want to have a successful business, you cannot be dependant on any one source of leads. You must have multiple lead generation techniques working for you at all times. You will have a hard time trying to find just one home run method.

It is far easier and more realistic to find a few methods that consistently hit singles and doubles. Let me use a story to clarify my point. There was a successful doctor who built a million dollar practice, sold it, then built another one, sold it, then built a third. At a seminar he was asked by another doctor, "Can you give me a technique so I can get 100 new clients?" The doctor answered, "I don't know 1 way to generate 100 new clients, but I know 100 ways to generate 1 client."

Lead generation is what will keep you in business. Everything else is secondary. You can have the best rates, millions of lenders or be the most lenient lender in the world, but without leads you will be out of business before your next birthday.

If you get nothing else out of this book, get this: YOU CAN NEVR STOP GENERATING LEADS. They are the life blood of your business. They are the future commission checks you dream about at night. They are the ticket to your financial independence. If you have enough leads, even if you are the worst loan officer working at the worst company, you will still make a living.

Without leads there is no way to improve your business. If you have leads, everything else can be improved.

ADVERTISING METHODS

There are a zillion ways you can market to the masses.

There are two main ideologies in prospecting. The first is to go to the customer. The second is to get the customer to come to you. Which is easier? It is easier to go to the customer. But this results in fewer sales. When the customer comes to you, you will have a much easier time converting the prospect into a client. And that is the type of marketing and prospecting you should focus on.

Ask yourself this question. How do I identify people who want a loan? We call this getting your prospects to raise their hands.

Have you ever been fishing? If you have, you know that it can get pretty complicated. Bait, lures, time of day, and most of all—location. Knowing how to market is a lot like fishing.

- You have to know where your prospects are.

- You have to get their attention with a lure.

- You have to offer them bait that they like.

- You have to let them bite on the bait at their leisure.

- You set the hook during the interview.

- You reel them in slowly during the loan process.

- Lastly, you land them at closing.

But you won't find any prospects if you don't go to where they are. And that is the hardest part of the game. If you know where the fish are and that they are hungry, it doesn't matter what bait you use or even if you have a lure. They will bite at anything.

In our scenario we want to find the right prospects. That is what prospecting is all about.

Image advertising is the same as putting your line in the water and waiting for a bite. The more lines you put into the water the better your chances of getting a bite, but it can get real expensive. And this is the type of marketing most mortgage companies use.

If you were looking for a mortgage company, would it matter to you if the company was around for twenty years, or if they have a well designed logo? Probably not. You would want a mortgage company that made it easy to do business with them, and that gave you what you wanted.

When you see an ad where you cannot even identify what is being sold, that is an image ad. Advertising agencies push this type of advertising to "create brand awareness". The truth of the matter is that this type of advertising is not trackable. And therefore you can never tell if it is working or not.

But if you change your approach and use the right lure, you can get the prospects to come to you. You can get them to call you and say, yes, I am interested in getting a loan. This is what direct response marketing is all about.

The ultimate goal of prospecting and marketing is to get the prospects to do something.

In most cases, this means moving that prospect from the education and consideration stage to the application stage. Direct response marketing can do just that. A direct response ad works when you get a response. No response, bad ad. It's as simple as that. When you need a flood of leads quickly, you use direct response. When you want to fill your funnel with prospects, you use direct response.

NICHE

We have already talked about niche marketing. So you already understand the benefits. Once you identify your niche you need to determine what they want. That is all they are interested in. Consumers could care less what you want. If you want their business, you first have to give them what they want.

Once you identify what they want, find a creative way to offer it to them. Let's refer back to my coaching client who serves the niche market of motorcycle owners. He owns two and he loves everything to do with them. And in case you didn't know, a motorcycle like a Harley Davidson can cost tens of thousands of dollars. The people who own these machines are not the biker gang thugs from the stereotype anymore.

What my client does is visit all the dealerships in his area. He talks to the salespeople and offers to help them sell more bikes. If anyone comes to them and cannot afford a bike or qualify for a loan, the bike salesperson loses the sale. But if they have some equity in their home, my client can get that equity out so they can buy the bike. They sell more bikes, and he gets motivated prospects. He can also keep track of how many clients each salesman and dealership sends him.

This is a clear case of choosing a niche, finding what the niche wants (a new bike), and finding a way to help them get it.

THE THREE PILLARS

In your Marketing Plan there will be three pillars you will market to. An effective plan address all three pillars and works to generate leads and business from all three. They are:

1. Consumers

2. Real Estate Agents

3. Businesses

CONSUMERS

This pillar is the easiest to target and the first one most loan officers go after. The consumer pillar consists of all consumer oriented marketing. This includes but is not limited to:

- Your website

- Refinance ads

- FSBO's

- Most of your referral efforts

- Direct Response Advertising

REAL ESTATE AGENTS

This pillar is to generate leads from your agent partners. Agents are still a very valuable asset to have on your team. Maintaining relationships with a few can provide a stable stash of leads every month.

BUSINESSES

The business pillar can be an extraordinarily strong source of leads if marketed to and approached properly. Business owners are looking for the same thing you are: more business. By joining forces and creating alliances, you expand your marketing reach exponentially.

The business pillar includes:

- Referrals from other financial based professionals: financial planners, accountants, bookkeepers, title agents, stock brokers, lawyers, etc.

- Endorsed mailings with other businesses

- Cross promotion of other businesses

Here's a real life example. As an active loan officer, my father uses all three pillars to generate leads. To attract consumers, he uses our Greed Stimulator System, which brings him homebuyers before they go to the realtors. He also uses our Referrals on Demand System to continue to expand his database and generate several referrals each month.

To generate realtor business, he used our Marketing to Real Estate Agents Toolkit to get realtors to call him. Since he has already built up relationships with several realtors, he does not need to approach new ones. He focuses mainly on cementing the relationships he already has.

Business wise, he is involved in a few local associations and chamber of commerce activities, as well as being active in our local church. He has formed relationships with a financial planner, two accountants, and a couple others. They refer their clients to each other when the need arises. He also does endorsed mailings occasionally.

As you start to Jump Start Your Career, your focus should be on the consumer pillar. But know that you cannot only depend on one pillar to have a strong business. The other two pillars are more difficult to break into, but once you do, the results are long lasting and very profitable.

Your success in all three pillars is dependant on your marketing and lead generation skills. The more leads you generate, the more people in your network, the more others will search you out, wanting to work with you. This includes realtors and other referral partners.

What To Do First

If I were starting out all over again, here is what I would do. First, I would make a list of all the lead generation techniques I know and have seen others use. Some ideas are given in the next few chapters. I would list them all and make notes as to their cost, number of people they reach, and possible response.

Second, I would choose three consumer pillar lead generation techniques. By choosing the most cost effective of the three I give myself a good chance of success. But I also have to keep my marketing budget in mind. I would track all three closely to see where my leads are coming from and of what quality they are.

Third, I would plan out my marketing calendar. What days do I do what? For how many hours? My marketing activities will be penciled into my day planner in advance. This ensures that my marketing will get done, no matter how busy I get.

Fourth, as the leads come in, I would work on my lead conversion skills and try to convert as many leads into interviews.

Fifth, I would try to automate the lead generation process as much as possible. I want to make sure the marketing gets done, but not have to do it myself. I would use a website, email, fax, regular mail, voice mail, and other technologies to get the job done for me.

Sixth, I would refine and fine tune the three techniques I am using. If they are not working properly I would drop them and try something else. And then I would continue to add more techniques one at a time until I was generating enough leads to be happy.

DON'T DO WHAT EVERYONE ELSE IS DOING

Look around at the advertising most loan officers do. Look at the advertising of most mortgage companies. If you remove the name of the company, can you distinguish one offer from another? Probably not.

One of the biggest mistakes new loan officers make is to copy exactly what other loan officers are doing. And that is a great way to go, if the loan officer copied was successful. But more often than not, that's not the case. Don't use any of these approaches.

"Everybody is doing this." Don't choose the most common advertising method just because you see others in the industry doing it. You do not know their results. If everyone is doing it, then why aren't they all successful?

"It was easy to do." Don't choose the method that is easiest to implement. Having your name in the yellow pages is easy to do, but will it get you clients?

"I just want to get my name out there." Don't leave your advertising budget to chance. Make sure every dollar counts and is tracked. If your advertising is losing money, change it or try something else.

AVOID PEAK AND VALLEYS

In order to be truly effective with lead generation you must have a plan, a budget, a message, and a target market. Too many loan officers base their marketing on something they heard in the latest seminar or in the newest fad book. This idea-of-the-month marketing is why loan officers experience peaks and valleys.

A peak is a good month when as a loan officer you have several leads and closings. A valley is when you have nothing closing and few prospects.

Let's take the example of a typical loan officer named Jack. Jack starts off Month #1 all pumped up. He has been studying marketing and has some great ideas he wants to implement. After a few weeks, his marketing starts to generate interest. He now has leads to work on. Slowly those leads turn into loan applications.

Month #2: Things look good. Jack is busy. When business is good, Jack slacks off on his marketing. He has other important things to take care of. "Did the McGrady appraisal come in?" "Can we get Lopez approved as a stated income?" Getting these loans closed is the most important thing to Jack at this moment.

After a couple weeks, Jack closes 3 loans. Payday! Jack feels good about himself. Two of the loans almost fell through. Now it's Month #3 and once again Jack has no prospects. So he goes back to the marketing he did in Month #1.

- In Month #1—Jack had no income.

- Month #2—3 closings.

- Month #3—No income.

Let's not be like Jack.

Your lead generation activities need to be constant. Today's lead is tomorrow's loan. You cannot sacrifice tomorrow's loan for today's. You need them both. As you plan your marketing, make sure you are always generating leads. Make sure you are always prospecting for new business. This will ensure that you will always have loans in the funnel.

THE FUNNEL

This is a term used to describe the process a lead takes through your marketing system. The funnel is to be wide at the top and narrow at the bottom. Leads go into the top, and closings come out of the bottom. As a lead makes its way through the funnel it goes through several stages.

These stages will be determined by your follow up and conversion strategies. As you get a lead, you can start them on an email follow up campaign or a postal letter campaign.

Each step along the funnel takes them closer and closer to the closing. Each point of contact is geared and created to take them to the next level.

Realistically, you will have people leave the funnel. That's ok. As long as you have enough leads going into the funnel you will have enough closings at the bottom. By knowing your numbers you will know exactly how many leads you need to put into your funnel every month.

The number one reason of failure amongst loan officers is lack of business. Generating leads is not easy, and many loan officers never understand how crucial it is. That is why they never bother to thoroughly study the art of prospecting. If you want to avoid their fate, you must become a student of marketing.

Everything starts with a lead. Without a lead, you have nothing. Everything else is easy. What sets apart the million dollar earning loan officers from the failures is the number of leads they get. Never lose focus of this fact.

CHAPTER 12

CHEAP MARKETING

Now for generating leads cheaply and quickly.

Marketing does not have to be expensive. The best marketing ideas can cost the least.

When starting out, your best tool is desperation. Others call it motivation. When you have three kids and no money for food, you will do what it takes to advance. That is exactly the mentality you should have, especially when you start out.

Your focus must be on marketing. Sure, there is plenty to learn and do. But you MUST start marketing yourself on Day 1. That's the only way to generate business, to make money. And that is why you got into this field, right?

This chapter shows you how to generate leads cheaply. Keep this in mind: When you don't have money, you must invest time. As you get busier, you will spend money instead of time, but the marketing must continue. You can never stop marketing. NEVER.

1. Talk to your clients.

One of the best ways to increase revenue is to talk to your existing clients. Ask five to ten clients if they'd participate in a phone interview. Tell them you need honest answers and that whatever they say will not affect your relationship or friendship. For the best results, consider having someone else do the interviews.

Have the interviewer ask value-based questions such as:

- What problems were you trying to solve when you considered using my services?

- How important were my services in solving your problems or addressing your challenges?

- What did you value most about my work?

- What did you feel was the reason you chose me as your loan officer?

- What could I have done better?

- What was the most important criterion in choosing a loan officer?

- What was the thing you liked most about my services?

After completing the interviews, compile the information to spot trends and themes.

Make sure to send a thank-you letter to every client who participated. Explain what you learned from the interviews and what changes you plan on making to serve your clients better.

Be careful how you ask the questions. Don't fire away. The interviewer should engage in a conversation and gather valuable data. Remember, it's not about how satisfied they are—it's about how much they valued your service.

You do not have to wait until they become clients. You can ask such questions while they are prospects. Getting to know what your prospects really want in a loan officer will help you convert them into an application.

2. Creatively package your marketing campaigns.

How about filling a small box with a fork, knife, spoon, and printed napkin that invites your prospect to "have lunch on us?" Think outside the box, and your marketing campaigns will have more impact.

Look at other industries to see what they are doing. What is working for them? Adapt that to your business. Who knows who came up with the drive-thru window? It sure was a brilliant idea. Just check out fast food restaurants, banks, dry cleaners, even pharmacies. They all use it.

3. Get the word out with publicity.

You do not need to hire a high-priced public relations company. You can do the PR yourself. Although a good firm brings solid contacts and experience, most loan officers can do enough PR on their own to spark the public's interest.

PR is free and more credible than any advertising you can do. That is why it is so powerful. And it is easier to get than you think. In the Jump Start Online Course, there is a whole section on PR and how to get it.

The first step is to generate a press release. Next up is getting that release distributed and read. Keep improving your releases. Make them interesting, and people will pick them up.

Don't expect one story placement to generate thousands in revenue. Your success depends on leveraging each press release and published article. Put everything on your website. Create a news page and add a What's New area on your home page. Keep adding to your marketing kit and sending items to clients, colleagues and professional organizations. Include a note in your newsletter that says "Recently Seen In..."

And remember: PR is more cost-effective and more credible than advertising.

4. Leverage existing relationships.

Most people know at least 300 people. Do the math: If you know 300 people and they each know 300 people, that's 90,000 potential contacts! Spend time developing relationships with the people you know—clients, colleagues, people you meet through professional networking organizations, friends, and even family.

Marketing to the people you know is the most cost-effective marketing you can do. It is also the most effective. Relationship Marketing, also known as Database Marketing, is the cornerstone of getting referrals. If you want to get more referrals, the easiest way is to increase the size of your database and your marketing and service to it.

Start by making a list of all the people you know. Next, prioritize your list into A's, B's and C's.

A's are your advocates. These are the people who feel strongly about you. They're the cheerleaders who would refer business to you right now.

B's could become advocates if they knew more about you, so you need to educate them.

C's are people you don't communicate with often enough. You'd have to nurture them before they'd refer any business your way.

The business and referrals will come once you fill your database with people who like and trust you. The key here is to build friendships. Scout for ways you can help your database. Start from the perspective of giving more than you ask for, and your database will become your most valuable marketing tool.

5. Email marketing.

Just about everyone has an email account. And it is free to send as many as you want. Jump on this medium—especially since many professionals access their email more than their voice mail.

Marketing through email is flexible, cost-effective, easy to measure (assuming you put the right tracking in place), and high impact. It lets you easily drive traffic to your website, reach a broad geographic audience and stay in frequent contact with your customers and prospects. Email marketing lets you market your services *and* establish your expertise with your audience.

The best use is to stay in touch with your database. You should often send out an email newsletter along with a print newsletter. Include announcements about new products and business successes.

Keep track of all the laws. Don't spam people, sending them stuff they don't want. And keep your emails interesting to your database. They shouldn't be all about you or the mortgage business. Most people don't care what the rates are unless they are looking for a home. So give them information they can use.

6. Use your imagination.

I saw a realtor's ad the other day, and the agent's name was Lester. His website was www.lesterthelister.com. Sounds kind of corny, but it will get noticed, and people will remember it.

Imagine a mailing that comes as a bank money bag, a printed paper bag, or a lumpy mail pack that has a silver platter in it with a sales letter to correspond. Or a letter that comes delivered inside a clear plastic bottle.

These are all low-cost tactics that will wake up customers and prospects.

Brainstorm how you can use your imagination to market your product or service. As they say, "You are only limited by your imagination."

Imagination can make your marketing fun. Involve customers and prospects. Put energy and enthusiasm behind your ideas, and you'll soon have your market talking about your imagination and, eventually, your products and services.

7. Offer something for nothing.

One of the biggest ways to draw a crowd off- and online is by offering something for free. In particular, something of interest to your target market. For loan officers, that something is information. The best thing about information is it can be packaged cheaply and has great value.

If you want to market to rich folks, consider a seminar on how to buy a second home—how to choose the city and deal with the tax ramifications. If your market is first-time home-buyers, offer a list of down-payment assistance programs.

When you provide such freebies, people will flock to you. Some may want only your free stuff, but many will see you as the expert. This will result in them coming back to you for more help and eventually a loan.

8. Join online discussion groups.

Reams of online groups discuss everything. Included are people looking to buy homes who need your help.

Once you find a couple of groups, visit the forums and message boards. Respond to questions regarding your area of expertise. You should create a subtle signature file to post along with your responses. This file should direct people to your website for further information.

Some sites to target: groups.yahoo.com, groups.google.com, and groups.msn.com.

9. Consider the charitable angle.

People enjoy making a contribution to worthy causes and doing business with companies that try to improve the human condition. Consider setting aside a portion of all commissions as donations to a specific charity. Make sure to select a charity with a wide appeal and good reputation. Don't forget that these donations make hot topics for press releases, which could spark attention and sales.

Or, consider letting your clients pick the charity. Most of them have a favorite. Tell them in the initial interview that a portion of your fee will go toward that charity. For an added touch, you can make the donation in the clients' names.

10. Sell yourself as an expert.

People want to believe that you are an expert they can trust with their hard-earned cash. A home loan is a huge undertaking, and people do not want to make a mistake by choosing a loan officer they cannot trust or have no confidence in.

As a new loan officer, you must gain people's confidence. How? Emphasize any training programs you have taken. State that all your work will be reviewed by a senior loan officer. And underscore the number of loans you are working on (if it is more than three).

The best way to show confidence is by answering your clients' questions rapidly. If you don't know the answer, find out quickly. And study until you can answer 95% of all questions yourself.

If you are an experienced loan officer, speak publicly on your industry. Speakers are needed at trade shows, chamber of commerce functions, and high school/college career festivals. Speak at them, and you'll earn the expert tag.

Another way to position yourself as an expert is to become a part-time teacher in a college or community center. That way you can share your knowledge of business and your industry with others. Or write an e-book related to your niche. That could gain you considerable recognition as an author as well as revenue.

11. Teach at a real estate school.

By teaching at a local real estate school, you can meet dozens of real estate agents every week. And since they will see you as an expert, you have a good shot at their business.

12. Promote upcoming events on your answering machine.

If all you're doing on your telephone answering machine is expressing regret that you are not available to take a call, you're missing an important sales opportunity.

Keep your message fresh. Generate additional interest by mentioning upcoming events. Throw in new products, teleseminars, updates to your website, and your latest newsletter topics.

13. Make your bills pay.

We all have too many bills to pay. Why not make the dreaded process a marketing opportunity? Make sure to include your marketing material with every bill you pay. Get as many business cards out there as you can. You never know who is opening your mail.

14. Contests.

Contests generate excitement about your company because everyone likes to be a winner. A well-designed contest will increase traffic to your website, improve off-line and online visibility, and leave your customers feeling good, even if they don't win. Here are some tips for holding an effective contest:

1) Offer something worth winning. A significant and valuable prize won't cost much if it's related to your business.

2) Select the audience by selecting the prize. By choosing a gift that relates directly to your business, you'll attract only potential customers.

3) Offer consolation prizes. Knowing other prizes are in the pot makes people more likely to enter. You may want to offer an inexpensive prize to all entrants.

4) Think globally. Make sure your prize can be delivered anywhere.

5) Know the rules. Make sure there are no legal restrictions on awarding your prize to whoever might win it.

15. Choose an appropriate email address.

Prospects rely on numerous subtle details to judge your competence and attention to detail. Before you even open your mouth, your prospect will be evaluating you by analyzing details such as your email address. It can tell a lot about you.

Be especially careful if you have a free email address with Hotmail or Yahoo.

It's hard to take a Mercedes-Benz salesperson seriously after glancing at his card and seeing a free email address, especially one with a cute moniker.

16. Consider joining Business Networking International.

Do you hate to stand up and speak? Are you uncomfortable distilling the essence of your business to a 60-second infomercial?

If you answered "yes" to either question, you're probably a good candidate for joining a local chapter of Business Networking International. BNI is a nationwide firm with chapters throughout the country, in cities large and small. Chapters are limited in size, so you may have your choice of chapters in your area.

Each week, BNI members meet to share referrals and deliver a 60-second description of their own business. You'll be surprised at how your confidence will grow the more often you stand up and present. You may develop strong friendships while profiting from qualified business referrals.

To locate a chapter in your area, visit www.bni.com.

When attending a networking meeting, avoid the temptation to issue open-ended requests for referrals.

Wrong way: "I'm interested in anyone who wants to buy a new car," or "I'm interested in referrals to people who are going to sell their home."

Right Way: "I'm interested in an introduction to the marketing manager of Kamrock Publishing," or "I'd like to meet the individual in charge of HR or employee training."

By using this approach you'll get a much higher response to your requests. Others in the room may already know the individual. They might know others at the firm and will find out for you. In still other cases, they might not know the HR person at Kamrock Publishing, but they DO know the HR person at another, similar, firm in the area.

17. Handle rejection with grace.

It's hard to be gracious when a prospect tells you he went with another company. Many times, the prospect simply won't call back. Yet your grace under fire is important.

Recognize that by qualifying for the short list, you're in a rarefied atmosphere. Out of all the people in the world, you were one of the few who made the initial cuts!

Taking the time to thank your prospect for the opportunity of talking with him keeps you in the running for future opportunities. Circumstances change. The company selected may have made a better offer than you, but if it cannot back up its claims, the prospect might come back to you.

Then again, a prospect might want to come back but feels embarrassed about the way he didn't call back or tried to negotiate with you. By sending a thank-you letter, you leave the door open for that person to walk through. It also leaves a positive impression that can result in future business and referrals.

18. Define your business in terms of markets and benefits, not services.

When someone asks "What do you do?" you feel like describing the product or service you offer. That's natural because you're so close to the action. The problem is, this leads to weak answers. Such as: "I'm a loan officer with XVY Mortgage."

Better to couch your expertise in specific terms. Such as: "I help make the American Dream come true for new immigrants," or "I help seniors align their housing situation with their financial and retirement plans so they can retire sooner than expected."

Remember, we want them to ask us for more information about us.

19. Be an expert giving teleclasses.

Having expert status in the community is a great way to get more loans. Teleclasses are a great way to get your name out, be perceived as the expert, and maybe even make money.

Many loan officers do regular homebuyer seminars. You know how these work: run some ads, get people to come to your office or hotel, and talk to them for an hour or so, then try to get them to schedule an interview with you. And sometimes they work great. If you are a strong speaker and you match your ad message just right, you can get some really qualified prospects to come to you.

The downside is it costs money and a heck of a lot of time. Unless you do these regularly, they might not be worth it.

But what if you could do the same thing via phone?

Instead of renting hotel space, rent a bridge line. Prospects call you or go to your web page to register. At the proper time, you give your lecture on the phone. Your prospects can be listening on the other end. It's like a three-way call—with a lot more people. Maybe thousands are listening to you.

This costs less than normal seminars, takes a lot less time to set up and implement, and reduces the no-show factor. Added bonus: If you record the call, you can use it as a promotional piece.

Here's a sample marketing plan for a teleclass:

1) Rent a bridge line. It can cost $25. A bridge line is simply a phone line that will let many people call in at once. Here are some criteria to keep in mind when choosing a company.

Size of line: The more people who participate, the more you will pay. Try to find a company that will charge you only per-person calling in—not on the amount of people the line can hold. Also, you want your listeners to be calling a local line or toll-free line. Most don't want to call long distance.

Muting capability: You want the sound as clear as possible. Callers should hear only the person talking—not everyone on the line. You don't want people coughing, talking, or the TV going in the background during your call.

Recording capability: Do it yourself or have the line company do it for you. And have the firm provide you the recording in digital format, either MP3 or .WAV, so you can burn CDs and have the file play on your website.

2) Once you have your line picked out, choose your topic.

3) Then choose one of two class formats. 1. Only you can talk; or 2. You can talk some of the time, and people can ask questions some of the time.

Decide how long you will talk. Write your class notes on paper. Three minutes of speech equals one sheet of typed material. So if you want to talk for 30 minutes and you just read the material, you will need 10 letter-sized sheets of paper.

Decided whether your class will be free. Charging for it means more people who register will show up. But fewer people might register. It depends on what you are looking for— prospects or people seriously looking to do something right now.

4) Next, craft your ads. Write a headline for your class and five of the main benefits people will gain. If the class is free, your local newspaper might print your announcement for free. Use fliers, emails, and other cheap methods to get people's attention.

Decide how they will register. Do they have to contact you to get the phone number? I suggest yes. Get all their information before the call. This way, you can remind them of the call and can follow up afterward. Have them call your office or go to your website and fill out a form. Then provide them the phone number along with the date and time. Make sure to get their name, phone number, email, and address. Also try to gauge how serious they are. Do they want to move in one month? Three months? A year? If you are charging, you must have a way to accept payment.

You can advertise your call for free on a few websites, such as SeminarAnnouncer.com and TrainersLink.com.

5) On the day of the class, call participants to remind them of the call. Email reminders don't work as well here. Call them 15 to 30 minutes before the call and give them the phone number to call along with any access info they need. If you are giving the class, have someone else do this. Another option is do a voice broadcast to everyone who registered.

Present your lecture, and answer any questions. Again, make sure to record the call. The phone company should be able to help you with this. During the call, give them your Unique Selling Proposition a few times, your website address, and your phone number. At the end, offer them a free report or analysis. That could help them want to meet you.

20. Astounding salesletters.

When we first opened our mortgage company in Houston, we decided to do a mailing to a targeted group. On the top of the salesletter we attached a $1 bill. This campaign yielded an astounding 30% response rate. We used a real dollar-bill but you can use anything else. You can even use foreign currency which costs a lot less, is more colorful, and is seen as exotic.

It's all about grabbing attention. You simply want people to read your letter. If it takes something stuck to the letter, good.

21. Join an association.

Why do people join associations?

1) Social reasons. They want to create friendships and influences that may have otherwise taken years to build.

2) Promotional reasons. They want to offer their own products or services to others in a cost-effective and positive way.

3) Educational reasons. They want to see what others are up to and check out the latest developments in the marketplace.

Grow your network and your database by joining groups of established people. By socializing with people with whom you have common traits, you can generate business more easily. People like to do business with people they like and trust. People like others who have similar interests as they do.

22. Bookstores.

I often ask my coaching clients, "How can you tell if people need a mortgage? What do they do? How do they act?"

If you provide the right answers, you can easily be rich in the mortgage business. By spotting when they want a mortgage before they start looking for one, you can get a jump on all the other loan companies. This is one area of our business that annoys me. Most other businesses have a way to identify when people will need their service and can market to them accordingly. When people buy new homes, they buy furniture, blinds, the usual home accessories. So if we were selling any of these items, all we need is a list of new homeowners to market to. And that list is easily available. But how the heck do we figure out who is thinking of getting a mortgage?

One of my clients had a great answer: "They might go to the bookstore or library and buy books on home buying, mortgages, or real estate in general." And that's true. Every bookstore has a real estate section. And most of the books are for consumers buying and selling real estate.

My next question is, "Now that we have identified what they do, how do we get our message in front of them?"

My client again came to the rescue with this simple method: "Go to the bookstores and libraries and put a business card in each book."

After doing it for a couple of months, he learned that the best place to put the card was in the front. Try for the first chapter because not everyone reads the whole book.

Second, pick books with the best covers and graphics. They sell the best.

Third, not all books sell and some are sent back to the publishers, who might also see your card.

Fourth, having a USP on the card helps boost response.

Fifth, it takes just 10 minutes per bookstore.

Sixth, he averages four calls a month and one loan per month.

Seventh, he now has his assistant do it. And she goes once a week.

Eighth, the people who call are in search of more information, so offering them unbiased advice and more resources really turns them on.

If you have the time and are brave enough to do it in front of people, try it and see what you get. I wanted to test it in my market. So I went to three bookstores and put in 120 cards.

I got two calls, and one of them is a serious prospect. If I do it more often, I have no doubt it will work for me.

23. Orphan files.

When a loan officer leaves a company, the clients he/she brought to the company are called orphans. These clients now belong to the company. Ask your manager to see if you can contact orphans to see if they need mortgage or real estate help. Be nice enough, and they will let you add them to your database.

24. Go where the borrowers are.

Identify the demographics of your target buyers: age, sex, occupation, neighborhood, income, hobbies. Then market to them.

But you must have a marketing plan. You can't go after anyone and everyone. You need to determine whom to go after. This is called your niche. You will have much greater success going after a niche than the general public.

What do you enjoy doing? Swimming? Then join a swim club and offer members a way to afford their own pool-refi. Then contact pool builders and tell them how you can help them win over clients who think private pools are too expensive.

Do you like motorcycles? Contact all the dealers in your area and show them how you can help them sell more bikes by refinancing their prospects.

Any group passionate about its hobby is a great niche market. And easy to dominate.

Do you go to church? That's one of your niches.

If you used to be a financial planner, that's your niche. You can relate to planners. You talk their jargon. It's easy to get them to like you.

Organize your business, build systems, and map out plans. Only then will you be strong when the winds blow.

25. Trade Shows.

Another coaching client of mine goes to trade shows. Not the ones related to our business. He goes to electronic shows, design shows, car shows, and his favorite: women's trade shows.

Most of the time, he represents the only mortgage company there. Result: He averages three loan applications per show. The trick is to tie in your business with the show. At a car event, you can rev up this ad: You want a vehicle? I'll help you buy it.

If you can preapprove someone at a car show for a cash-out refinance, he can buy that hot car he's been salivating over the last two hours. Instant gratification.

26. Join a local real estate investment group.

All major cities have one. And each group is full of people buying and selling houses. They need money to buy houses, and they need money to help others buy their houses.

27. Realtor open houses.

Visit realtor open houses on weekends. Offer to leave some financing material.

When you get to know a realtor, you can offer to do open houses for her. She'll finally be able to take a break while you sit in her stead. It is not a fun way to spend an afternoon, but you might get a couple of leads.

If you go this route, make sure the house has serious traffic. And make sure the agent advertises and lends you signs and balloons. You do not want to sit in a ghost house—hard to find and off everyone's radar screen.

Another tip: Meet the neighbors of the home. See if they know anyone wanting to move or buy. Chances are someone will know of a family wanting to move into the neighborhood.

28. Realtor MLS.

Want a source of thousands of people who will be getting a mortgage within the next couple of months?

It's sellers. And the Multiple Listing Service used by realtors is full of them. Do a search of homes for sale, get the owners' names from the tax records and you have yourself a good prospect list.

Mail them something about you or an offer for free information. Call them if you can get their phone number and they are not on the Do Not Call list. Or drop by their house if you have the guts.

This is exactly what one of my coaching clients does. He calls realtors who have listings and asks them if he can market his services to the home sellers. Many realtors say yes. When they do, he contacts the sellers and tells them their realtor said he could call on them.

He tells me most home sellers he contacts open up to him. He gets several loans a month using this trick.

29. FSBO's

For sale by owners are also home sellers. Stop by every FSBO sign you see and check if the home seller needs any help qualifying the people that come to see his house.

You might create a package for FSBOs containing info about how to market and sell their house. Your package could include an offer for you to pre-qualify anyone wanting to make an offer on the property. That way the seller knows that whoever offers to buy can get financing.

If you can get the seller to fax you a list of people who visit the house, maybe on a weekly basis, that would be a great list of prospects looking to buy.

30. Walk for charity.

No doubt your town holds charity walks several times a year. Corral some of your family and past clients for a walk team. Its aim is to walk and raise money together. Make some cheap T-shirts displaying your name, USP, and website for your team to wear.

Thousands of people will see your team walking with the T-shirts. Add a banner for even more promotion. Get pictures taken and submit your accomplishment as a press release.

Your past clients will thank you for getting them involved. As for future clients, the free advertising will help. Then there's the charity, which will land money. Winners all around.

CHAPTER

MORTGAGE WEBSITES

According to a recent survey by the National Association of Realtors, 77% of homebuyers used the Internet to help their home search. It's a good bet they looked for mortgage information at the same time. Also figure that those numbers will increase yearly until nearly everyone is using the Internet to search for homes and loans.

So your issue is: "How do I get my website to be the most effective for me?"

A MEMBER OF THE TEAM

Your website is a tool. It should make your life easier. The best websites attract prospects, follow up with leads, convert prospects into pre-quals and then into applications, keep the realtors and builders and everyone else informed during the loan process, help with presentations, and manage data.

That's what you want: a website that runs your business.

The success or failure of your website depends on you. If you have a lousy website, but you can convince people to go to it, it will succeed. If you have the best, most expensive website in the world, but you cannot draw anyone to it, it will fail. In the end, your website lives and dies because of your marketing.

YOUR WEBSITE

How to set up a site? Let's count the ways. You can use templates, hire a web designer, pay a mortgage website design company, or use software to design it yourself. Consider these three tips.

Keep it simple.

You don't want the user to have to think too much. Design the website so that your words, navigation, and graphics clearly communicate the services you offer and where the visitor must go for information. Don't concentrate so much on a pretty website that you sacrifice content and ease of access.

Keep it dynamic.

Update your website regularly. The Internet reports on new things with blinding speed. Web surfers expect change; if they visit a site two or three times and don't see anything new, they are likely to stop visiting. Keep at least your home page zippy. Consider using one or more of the following:

- Today's date when last updated.

- News that relates to your business.

- Cool fact of the day/week.

- Joke of the day/week.

- Cartoon of the day/week.

- Contest/game of the week/month.

- Holidays/seasonal page decoration.

Do your own updates.
Save money by doing your website updates in-house. Make sure your site design lets you or an assistant add information to pages and create new pages using current ones as templates. Even if you hire a web designer, you or your staff should be able to make changes. Actually, it's easy. If you can use Word, you can fiddle with a webpage.

WHAT EVERY MORTGAGE WEBSITE SHOULD HAVE

What comprises a dream mortgage website? I came up with some requirements that I would want in my ideal website.

I should be able to:

- Afford it easily. It should pay for itself in less than one loan.

- Add pages to my site easily. I don't want to become an expert in html.

- Have several email addresses.

- Have loads of content (articles and information).

- Have my own domain name: www.mymortgage-company.com.

- Have visitors fill out pre-quals and complete 1003s on the site and have that information safe from thieves and hackers.

- Take that info and import it into my loan processing software easily.

- Be notified by email when someone fills out a loan app online.

- Be able to generate leads by offering free information in the form of several different reports or email classes.

- Be able to follow up with visitors via unlimited time-delayed emails. This will automate the follow-up process for me.

- Have the system automatically email all the parties involved in a loan (listing agent, selling agent, borrower, seller, builder) when the loan file is updated. This will stop agents and others calling me for loan updates. This will also show my professionalism and result in more referrals.

- Automatically email prospects with a Rate Alert when the interest rate they are looking for is hit.

- Make changes to the site for search engine optimization.

- Change the design of my site in seconds—with dozens of mortgage website templates to choose from.

- Have surveys and questionnaires.

- Have an email newsletter.

- Have pop-ups.

- Input all my rates and have them update automatically.

- Have several mortgage calculators that I can use for other applications as well.

- Send personalized email blasts to my lists.

- Provide pages on my site to my referral partners.

- Have a link exchange to generate links to my site.

- Sell others' products as an affiliate if I choose.

- Have scrolling text that will float across the screen.

- Have visitors 24/7 without fail.

- Have free phone support if I ever have a question.

- Track my visitors and give complete stats on where my visitors are coming from, what they do on my site, and for how long.

Keys to Online Success

We're well into the 21st century. The Internet is here. It's part of business. Loan officers know it and thus market their products and services online.

The Internet offers a world of advertising opportunities. Instead of having to spend tens of thousands of dollars on print campaigns and mailings, you can reach a huge audience on a shoestring budget.

Here are key steps to successfully marketing your business online.

Obtain a good domain name.

Before you establish a website for your business, you need a domain name. A domain name is the Internet address that allows computer users to find your website, such as www.Microsoft.com or www.BananaRepublic .com. Good domain names are difficult to obtain, as millions have already been purchased over the years. The most common domain names end in ".com" or ".net".

A .com name is crucial. When you tell people your domain name or if they read it on your business card, they will assume it ends with .com because that's so common. They will type in yourdomain.com. If your tag is .net or .org, you have a problem. People might not find you. They will find someone else. You can only hope they realize it is not you. So do your best to get a .com name.

Also: Don't place a dash in the name. JoeShmoe.com trumps Joe-Shmoe.com. Why? Because a dash makes it harder to remember and say. On the other hand, search engines like dashes. So if you create a great domain name, register it both ways—with and without the dash.

It's easy to check whether a domain name is available. Just go to www.whois.net. That site even lets you check domain names that have just expired and are available again.

As for cost, you shouldn't have to pay more than $10 a year to register a domain.

Other tips as you set up a domain name:

- Make sure it hasn't been trademarked by someone else (check www.uspto.gov).

- Make sure it's easy to spell.

- Make the name easy to remember.

As an individual loan officer, you should use your name as the domain. I have registered ameenkamadia.com even though I do not use it. Eventually I will. You want people to remember your name, so using it as the domain is a good idea.

Again, try your best to get a .com name. Thereafter, consider registering the .net and .org extensions as well. You do not want your competition stealing traffic by using your name with a .net or .org extension.

Another good idea for a domain name is to use words that people search for regularly. How do you find those words? Check out Yahoo Search at *http://inventory .overture.com/d/searchinventory/suggestion.*

HOW TO GET YOUR SITE DESIGNED

Several companies provide turn-key mortgage websites. Some of the packages are decent. Most are garbage. Not one company out there offers everything from my list above.

Websites are powerful tools. They should do whatever you want them to. If a company limits your use, what good is it? That is why many loan officers try to build their own sites. A one-word suggestion: don't.

I can tell you from experience that the process is no fun. Not to mention the fact it takes a lot of time and money.

I have talked to many loan officers who hire a web designer and tell her, "I need a mortgage website. Please make me one." This is definitely not the way to go about it.

If you decide to go this route, design your site on paper first. Determine where the navigation links will go, where the pictures will go, and what the text will say.

An easier course: Surf the Internet until you find a site you like. Make yours similar to that one. That's what I did with MortgageBrokerTraining.com. I found a site whose layout I liked and told my designer to make it like that one with a few modifications.

Now we constantly update and upgrade the site. And every couple of years we come out with a new design. Coming up with the layout is a tough job. I was lucky to find a site designed to do something similar to what I wanted.

You can find great, inexpensive web designers at *www.elance.com*. You can post your project and designers from around the world will bid on how much they will charge. You can review their work and choose one.

Coming soon: MortgageBrokerTraining.com will offer our own mortgage websites. They will have all the tools mentioned above and more. They will be "complete" sites. You do not need multiple sites for originating and lead generation. One site should do it all. If interested, you can get more info at our website.

OFFER WHAT VISITORS EXPECT

Prospects to a mortgage website want information and rates. They want to know why they should work with you, so it sure helps when your USP is displayed up front. They also want to see testimonials of your past clients. If they see people similar to them using you, they will use you as well.

Don't get fancy.

The latest web technology will not get you any more loans. The most important thing on your page is your copy. Words will make your sales, not graphics or moving objects. Focus on the copy.

Make sure your site is fast.

If your site takes too long to load, visitors will not wait. Web surfers are impatient. Grab their attention with speed, or you will lose visitors you worked so hard to get.

How to check your site's speed? Visit the Web Page Analyzer at *www.websiteoptimization/services/analyze*. It tells you how fast your page loads at different modem speeds.

If your site takes too long to load, check with your designer and web host to get it done faster. If you are doing it yourself, reduce the file size of graphics on your pages and decrease the number of files on your web page.

Design Resources

Here are sites where you can find articles and help in designing your website:

SitePoint: *www.sitepoint.com*

Builder.com: *www.builder.com.*

Useit.com: *www.useit.com*

WebMonkey: *www.webmonkey.com*

AnyBrowser: *www.anybrowser.com*

WebDeveloper: *www.webdeveloper.com*

NetMechanic: *www.netmechanic.com*

Marketing Your Website

Face it. The Internet is unstoppable. So you better move with this trend and market online. Without an online presence, you'll lose leads and prospects.

People are now searching for services through their computers instead of through the yellow pages. If your business isn't on the web, you're missing a bulk of your market.

Two types of marketing exist when it comes to websites: online and offline. A website needs both. You need to incorporate your website into all your marketing.

Offline marketing is everything you do to promote your site off the Internet. Placing your web address on all your printed material is offline marketing. Running an ad in a newspaper for your website is offline marketing.

Online marketing is exactly like any other type of marketing. It's built around the same triggers. The difficult part is rising above the crowd. This is where you want a well thought-out Internet marketing plan.

Build up your email list

One of the best and cheapest ways to sell online is through email marketing. It's a great way to communicate with customers and prospective customers. So do your best to collect email addresses from every visitor to your web site. Offer them something worthwhile for their email address—maybe a discount or free newsletter. Be sure you have set forth a Privacy Policy on your site describing how you will use personal information. And be sure you are up-to-date on laws affecting email marketing, such as the CAN-SPAM Act.

We use a service to capture emails for all our websites. It captures emails, asks questions, and even creates pop-ups. The information collected is then stored, and we can follow up with everyone who subscribes. You can find the names of the companies we recommend at *http://mortgagebrokertraining.com/resources.html*

SEND EMAIL NEWSLETTERS

Email newsletters can be effective communication tools for clients, prospects, and other key audiences. What are the hallmarks of an effective email newsletter? Here are six tips:

- Keep it reasonably short and to the point.

- Make it well designed and visually interesting. Include photos and graphics. Provide multiple links back to your website.

- Make it look professional. Don't have typos, a sloppy look, or broken links.

- Include an easy way for the viewer to contact you and to unsubscribe from your email list.

- Constantly test and track how your newsletter is doing.

- Create a page on your website for each newsletter that you do. This way new visitors can read all the back issues. Plus you have more content on your site.

USE COMPELLING OFFERS ON YOUR SITE

A compelling offer is a special package, piece of information, or item that your visitors will likely find valuable. So valuable, in fact, that they will be willing to complete a form on your site for the privilege of receiving it (at no charge). The purpose of the compelling offer is to capture sales leads.

You should put at least one compelling offer on every page of your site. If you want visitor inquiries that convert to new clients, give them a reason to interact with you. Providing targeted and unique offers is the most powerful reason I can imagine!

The kind of compelling offers you make on your site will depend on your market niche. If you specialize in working with first-time buyers, your site's compelling offers are going to differ from those found on a site focused on buyers interested in golf properties.

Here are examples of compelling offers targeted to first-time home buyers:

- **Negotiating Tips to Know Before Making Your Offer**
  Receive our special report on three critical negotiating tips that will help you win the home of your dreams for less.

- **How to Be First to the Best Listings**
  Join our "VIP Club" to beat others to hot new listings.

- **Avoid Financing Disasters Without Paying a Dime**
  A financing expert explains the differences between fixed and adjustable loans and which one may be best for your unique situation.

- **How to Buy Your First Home with No Money Down**
  Receive our special report on how to purchase your home with no money down.

And here are examples for buyers looking for homes on golf courses:

- **Tee Off on Us**
  Receive our special voucher to play nine holes on us at one of our fine area club courses.

- **Get Course Info from the Pros**
  Read our exclusive interviews with local pros as they share the in and outs of local courses.

- **How to Make Your Course Home Your Best Investment**
  Get our special report on which course properties experienced the greatest appreciation.

Each compelling offer is specific to its market niche. Also, each offer is framed in the form of an attention-grabbing headline. This is crucial, because you must get visitors' attention to read the offer or else they won't bite.

The law of reciprocity says that when you give something to someone, he usually wants to return the favor. Use this principle when making compelling offers.

Make sure your offer requires delivery via email or snail mail. In either case, you will need to gather contact information before you can make the delivery. Every compelling offer needs to be connected to a form that the visitor completes in order to receive the item of value.

Keep this point in mind: Don't force visitors to fill out more information than they need to receive the item. Requiring mailing information for a downloadable document, for example, can seem suspicious and call your trustworthiness into question. However, do give them the option to tell more about themselves, their contact information, and what their interests and concerns are. You may be surprised how much people will share with you online if your site approaches them the right way.

Any compelling offer on your site needs to contain the following elements:

- Targeted to a specific niche market.

- Is considered extremely valuable by members of your target market.

- Is unique to you (i.e., only you are offering it).

- Uses an attention-grabbing headline.

- Uses a request form that invites visitors to share their information, yet assures them it will be kept private.

GETTING PEOPLE TO YOUR SITE

The best way to draw people to your site is via search engines. Close to 80% of traffic is driven by search engines. So use them.

OPTIMIZE YOUR SITE FOR SEARCH ENGINES

Hundreds of millions of searches a day are performed on the web through Google, Yahoo, and other engines. They "spider" billions of web pages. This process has spawned "search engine optimization," which refers to efforts you can employ to get your web site to show up higher in search results.

In order to land traffic from search engines, your site must rank high. Many times, if you are not on the first page, no one will click on your site.

So how to get on that first page? Search engines use evolving criteria to determine which site is No. 1 for a given search. If you want your site to be No. 1, it must be optimized for these criteria.

An entire industry called Search Engine Optimizers has been created to get sites the top rankings. Good SEO companies charge several thousand dollars. The price is right if the company knows what it is doing. How can you make sure? Ask any SEO company for names of previous customers and see how those sites rank in search engines.

I hired a company to help me with MortgageBroker Training.com. We went from not even existing on Google to being in the top five for over a dozen keywords. This stuff works if you hire someone to do it for you. There is no way you can optimize your site and still pay attention to your mortgage business. Remember, the website is only one tool of many.

ADVERTISING

Online advertising is cheap. Advertising in the phone book or newspaper is expensive, especially if you want an ad that has any presence on the page. An ad in an Internet directory is free on many sites, and you can put links directing customers to your website for more information. And because you can provide customers with a wealth of information, they no longer have to pick up the phone to get their questions answered.

Before you begin seeking out advertising avenues, develop an advertising budget. If you don't have the funds to wage a large-scale campaign, don't panic. There are many online advertising options that are inexpensive and effective.

Next, consider where you want to place your ads. If you target a niche, do some research and buy ads on sites that offer products or services that tie in with what you sell. If you need to reach a wide variety of people, a popular general interest web site would be the best place to start.

Here are three of the most popular online advertising strategies:

> **Link exchanges** can be great, especially if your advertising budget is limited (or nonexistent). Find merchants that sell complementary products, and offer to trade text links or ads with them. If you're starting out and your site doesn't get a lot of traffic, you may not get a one-to-one trade; be prepared to make concessions, at least until you have a track record—and traffic—to

point to. That said, most companies won't turn down an opportunity for more exposure, so you'll probably find a few willing to exchange links with you.

Newsletter advertising is a great way to reach select groups of consumers. If you target health nuts, you could advertise in a newsletter that offers health tips and advice. Because newsletter advertising is targeted, it can be cheaper than advertising to the masses. If your budget is tight, you can always start your own newsletter campaign.

Budgeted advertising, such as Google AdWords, lets you purchase a set of keywords, set a limit on how much you want to spend, and have your ad displayed until that limit is reached. This is a particularly useful way to track your campaign success, and has been a boon to small business owners.

No matter which avenue you take, give serious thought to your "creative"—the ad itself. Whether it's a text link or a banner-ad campaign, the creative can make or break your advertising initiative. Try several variations, track them, and see which ones perform best.

Budgeted advertising can be broken down into three categories:

- **Cost per click,** where you pay for actual clicks or leads for your advertising.

- **Cost per impression,** often referred to as cost-per-thousand impressions, where you purchase a set amount of views for your ad.

- **Set-price advertising,** where you can purchase a specific amount of advertising for a given length of time.

Cost-per-click advertising offers small business owners great value for their advertising dollar. There are several sites that offer the ability to pay only when customers click on your ads.

Google AdWords is one of the most popular advertising venues for small businesses. With the AdWords program, you bid on keywords related to your business, and your text ad is displayed when Google users search for that term. You pay only when a user clicks on your ad, and the cost per click varies according to the popularity of the keywords you select. Google AdWords does not require a minimum purchase, and you can easily spend less than $25 for a successful advertising campaign by utilizing AdWords properly.

Yahoo Search (formerly called Overture) is another leading provider of cost-per-click advertising. Overture, which is owned by Yahoo, displays ads on a network of major search engines and portals, including CNN.com and, of course, Yahoo.

MSN has a pay-per-click system as well.

Many other pay-per-click search engines want your business. But they normally are not worth the bother. The clicks just don't add up, and the visitors are not of the same quality. Two that I tried for MortgageBrokerTraining.com were goclick.com and enhance.com. We landed some clicks, but no orders. Absolutely zero. The problem was not the products or the copy. The response rates from our Google and Yahoo ads were great. The only reason I could find was that the people who use these other engines are not really that serious.

Cost-per-impression advertising is waning in popularity, but it can still be an effective way to advertise your business. These ads are usually in the form of banners or buttons, and are sold by cost-per-thousand impressions or displays of your ad. This means that if you purchase 5,000 impressions, your ad will appear 5,000 times. There are no click guarantees, which makes this type of advertising less popular than pay-per-click advertising options. Most cost-per-impression ad campaigns have steep minimum buys, which also makes them less attractive to loan officers just starting out.

Set-price advertising includes running ads in newsletters, text ads, and premier listings in directories. This can be compared to advertising in your local newspaper. You may be charged per line of text or a set amount determined by the publisher of your ad. Newsletter publishing is a great way to reach a targeted audience relatively cheaply. (Newsletter advertising may also be sold on a cost-per-click or cost-per-impression basis.)

Getting click-throughs is one thing, but also consider your ad's landing page—which your customers see when they click your ad. Simply dumping users on your home page isn't enough. Do everything you can to help users find what they want fast. If they can't, they will leave the site, and your money will be wasted. Make specific landing pages for specific ads so visitors will follow the prompts.

CREATING A CAMPAIGN

An ad campaign often features more than one of the approaches above and sometimes will utilize all three kinds of advertising. If your advertising budget allows it, try several kinds of advertising and see which performs best. No matter what advertising you employ, insist on performance data. Without that information, you will never know which advertising is effective.

It's obvious by now that it takes more than information to engage website visitors. They need a reason to make the initial

inquiry, and it's up to you to give it to them. Most people looking for real estate information do so with every intention of
being passive. Turning a passive visitor into an active one
takes something special, something compelling, something
that has a direct benefit to the visitor.

A website can be a great tool in your marketing arsenal.
But like all the others it requires time and effort. There are
many great resources online that can show you how to promote your website.

One final tip: You must own your own domain name. That
way, if you switch web hosts or providers you do not leave
your traffic behind.

A Turn Key Solution

As a loan officer, your focus should be on your business
not on your website. Learning all the nuances of building and
marketing a website is a full time job. And even then you
might not be too successful at it since mortgages is such a competition rich area online.

So I am in the process of making it easy for all loan officers
to have a website with all the tools they need, and a way that
they can market it on autopilot. Our company is working with
a web design firm to bring to the market the best mortgage
websites available that are affordable, that help you run your
business, and that actually bring you customers.

If you know anything about websites, you know that once you have one you have to then market it or no one will use it. I want to provide websites that have all the tools so that you as a loan officer can set it up once, and let it run.

If you need a great looking site, that will allow you to work more efficiently and generate clients for you, this is something you should look into. Visit our site and sign up to be notified when these sites are available.

CHAPTER 14

HOW TO HAVE REAL ESTATE AGENTS EATING OUT OF YOUR HAND

Real estate agents can be great partners to work with. Many loan officers make great livings by working only with real estate agents. On the other hand, many successful loan officers do not work with any real estate agents, either because they don't know how to get them, or they tried and found it was too difficult.

REAL ESTATE AGENT MENTALITY

The real estate agent knows that every loan officer would love to work with him. He knows that he controls the buyer. According to a nationwide survey, 70% of all homebuyers get their loan from the lender recommended by the real estate agent.

REAL ESTATE AGENT CONCERNS

The number one thing the real estate agent wants is for the deal to go through. He doesn't want to hear excuses if the contract expires or the buyer didn't qualify for the loan. Even if the loan is difficult, if you can do the loan, great; if not, he will take the buyer somewhere else. In reality, the real estate agent is at the mortgage industry's mercy when it comes time to getting paid. No closing, no commission.

Most real estate agents already work with at least one lender.

REAL ESTATE AGENT TRAINING

While the real estate agent is being trained, he is taught to give the buyer options about a lender when asked. This way the real estate agent cannot be held responsible if the lender screws up. When a buyer asks a real estate agent for a recommendation for a lender, most agents are taught to give three options to the buyer. The buyer is then free to call all three companies to secure the best loan and to make up his own mind of where to get his loan.

Not all agents follow this method. Some only recommend one, some two some none.

Whenever you work with a real estate agent, you want them to recommend you only. Why create more competition for yourself?

WHY WORK WITH REAL ESTATE AGENTS?

The fastest way for a loan officer to generate business and clientele is having large numbers of prospects come asking for loans.

Basically there are two main ways to get loans.

1. By referral—where someone actually tells another person to do business with you.

2. By marketing directly to the people who need a loan.

Generating customers by referral is a much easier and cheaper process than marketing for prospects. If you get a customer as a referral, most of the work has been done for you. Someone else sends them to you and they already have a good feeling about you even before they have met you. Whoever sent them to you has put their own integrity on the line by saying that you provide good service. This creates a good impression in the mind of the prospect.

If you do not have anyone to refer business to you, then you need to market your services in order to bring prospects to you. Once you provide excellent service, then perhaps these customers will start sending you referrals.

If you just compare these two forms of marketing (asking for referrals is still a form of marketing), working by referral has many more benefits.

- less cost

- less time wasted on people who cannot qualify

- higher conversion rate since the prospects were told about you from a trusted friend

- higher commissions

The best sources for multiple referrals are real estate agents. They do their own marketing and try to attract as many homebuyers to them as possible. They spend the money for us. They establish the relationship and then use the trust developed to recommend us. If we provide good service to the consumers and keep the agents happy, then it is in their best interest to keep sending us loans.

The hard part has always been to get the good real estate agents to send you loans. If they were easy to get business from we would all be rich. Over time, real estate agents have learned that mortgage people will jump through hoops to earn their business. And many make us do so.

- Nearly every mortgage company markets to real estate agents.

- Real estate agents have developed the mentality that we work for them instead of with them for the consumer.

- Some real estate agents can and do make life miserable for loan officers.

But all is not hopeless. There are a few ways to get around these shortcomings.

First of all, not all real estate agents are so shortsighted. There are many who honestly believe in providing true service to the consumer. And they are looking for the best service they can get from a mortgage company for their clients.

Second, there are so many agents out there that you do not need to work with the jerks. You will not have the time to work with every real estate agent. Nor should you. Many will not do the volume of business you want and others will be so hard to please they will drive you nuts. But if you focus on quality for the consumer and for the agent, you will be able to attract several good producing real estate agents to your team.

For illustration purposes let's use an example of you working with an agent that provides you with only one loan per month. Now keep in mind that this is very low and most do better than this. But if one agent provides you with one loan per month, that equals twelve loans a year. Multiply twelve by your average commission and this real estate agent is worth at least $12,000 a year in commissions to you. (If you make less than $1,000 per loan, you won't last long in this business).

If you help this person become better at what he does (if he only does one sale a month he is not doing very well), then you can double his income and help yours as well. And this does not include any other real estate agents that he refers to you. Once you become good at these partnerships you will have other agents calling you, wanting to work with you. But before you get to that stage you need to set up the relationships and mold them into partnerships.

Let's break down the numbers into easily digestible portions so that you can see the power of working with real estate agents.

How much do you want to earn?

Let's say you want to earn $100,000 and your average commission per loan is $1,500.

That means you'll need sixty-seven loans to reach your goal. Divided by twelve that's six loans a month.

Note: The prospects the real estate agents will refer to you will already be 90% sold on you. You will have to do very little convincing to get their loan. And they are less likely to shop their loan. That allows you to make a higher commission than from someone who just walked in off the street. So your average commission should be higher from referrals than from your other loans.

If your average real estate agent only generates two loans a month for you, you only need three real estate agents working with you.

Please notice that we only counted the loans that the real estate agents specifically gave us. These are the people the real estate agent is currently working with to sell a house. We did not count all the dozens of leads these agents will provide you of people who are interested in doing something, but need some convincing to use you and this real estate agent.

National statistics have shown that the average mortgage broker can convert one out of four qualified leads into a loan. That means that 25% of all the serious leads these agents give to you will become loans.

So if the average real estate agent does not provide any loans, but can provide just four leads a month, that would be more than one loan for you from that agent. And if an agent cannot produce even four leads a month, from open houses, floor time, referrals, ads, or anywhere else, then that person has no business being in his line of work.

Most loan officers think that getting real estate agents to work with them is hard, torturous, grunt work. It can be if you don't have the proper system. But with the proper system, if can be a breeze. Let me explain.

One of the products we have for sale at our website is called the Marketing To Real Estate Agents Toolkit. I want to show you the results we got from the system the first month we put it in action.

We mailed a newsletter (which is only one of the ways to attract agents and is included in the system) to 1,000 real estate agents. In the newsletter we advertised a free information package for real estate agents. All they had to do was call our office. Once they called, the receptionist scheduled an interview in the real estate agent's office so we could go and deliver the package and spend thirty minutes going over it with them.

Out of 1,000 newsletters mailed, we got 50 calls. From those 50 calls, not everyone wanted an interview and many were not worth an interview, so we were able to schedule only 34 appointments. Out of those 34 appointments we were able to meet with 26 real estate agents. Others canceled or never showed up.

26 out of 1,000. It doesn't sound very impressive does it? But remember, we do not need very many real estate agent partners to make a lot of money. Let's see the results.

Out of those 26 real estate agents, 14 committed to working with us right away, 5 more started doing business with us in month 2, and 1 started doing business with us in month 3.

In the first 3 months since we sent out the newsletter, directly referred to us by these real estate agents, we got:

- 5 loans in month 1

- 9 loans in month 2

- 8 loans in month 3

What I learned from the interviews was:

6 of 26 real estate agents were wary about recommending a mortgage company.

14 of 26 real estate agents were not very happy with any particular mortgage company.

5 of 26 had great relationships with a particular mortgage company.

7 of 26 sent all their clients to the in-house mortgage company.

But every real estate agent we met with was impressed with the material we presented and stated that they had never been approached by a mortgage company in such a professional way before.

Once again, let me point out that you do not need to work with dozens of real estate agents, and you don't need to market to every real estate agent in town.

WHAT YOU SHOULD NOT DO TO ATTRACT REAL ESTATE AGENTS

Beg for business: Continuing to harass a real estate agent to give you a chance is not going to help your cause. Agents don't want to work with needy loan officers. They want to work with the best so that all their deals close. By constantly asking and asking you will make yourself an enemy instead of a friend.

Whenever you approach a real estate agent you should provide some value or benefit for them. They should get something out of it so that you don't seem like a common loan officer.

Bribes don't work well either. On any given day in real estate agent offices across the country, uninvited loan officers show up carrying donuts, pizza, drinks, and other food items to get face to face with real estate agents. They think that by feeding the real estate agents, they can get their contact info and tell them about themselves. Plus if the real estate agent has a deal he is working on right now, the loan officer will offer to help with it right then and there.

But guess what? Only the real estate agents that have no business are the ones sitting around the office! The ones making all the money are out meeting clients, viewing and showing properties, or going to closings.

I'll let you in on a little real estate agent secret. When I was a real estate agent with Coldwell Banker, and I had just started, we encouraged loan officers that brought food to the office. There was a group of us, about six, that would meet at the office around 11 a.m., and wait for a loan officer to bring lunch. We had no intention of giving the loan officer a loan, mainly because we didn't have any to give. But we would make comments like, "Oh, you didn't bring any drinks? The guy from XYZ Mortgage didn't make that mistake, and he had pretty good rates, too." Most of the loan officers were new, so to make up for it, they would walk over to the Publix Supermarket, which was just a few doors down, and get a couple two liters of soda for us.

After a couple weeks of this, I started feeling guilty that I was taking advantage of these loan officers, so I stopped, but others in my office felt no such remorse. They might still be doing it to this day.

I am not saying that this tactic never works. I know many loan officers that have built their relationships primarily by feeding real estate agents. It might work for you, too. But chances are it will not work in the long run. If the first impression the real estate agent gets of you is a meal ticket instead of as a professional or a partner, there will always be tension in that relationship.

HOW DO YOU GET REAL ESTATE AGENTS TO WORK WITH YOU?

This is the million dollar question. And the answer is simply this: If you want someone to work with you, you need to show them why they should. You need to show them what's in it for them. How does working with you make their life easier, more enjoyable, less stressful, more rewarding? Why you and not every other loan officer that walks through the door?

In order to get real estate agents to work with you, you need to give them what they want.

SO WHAT DO REAL ESTATE AGENTS WANT?

It varies. Every real estate agent wants something different. Some want their loan officer to handle all details of the loan and closing and not be bothered with it. Others want to know every detail—what the rate is, when the appraisal will be done, the client's credit score, how much are you charging the client, etc.

Some real estate agents expect you to help them advertise. They want the loan officer to pay for any advertising that has them both listed. WARNING: This is actually a violation of the Real Estate Settlement Procedures Act (RESPA), so don't pay for the entire ad. Talk to your senior broker about what is and what is not acceptable.

I have met other agents who expect their loan officers to help them sell houses by holding open houses, or to immediately qualify any buyers they meet on Saturdays and Sundays.

But the one thing I found that every real estate agent wants is this: more customers! That's the reason we work with real estate agents, too, isn't it? The clients they can bring us? Well, agents are always looking for more clients, and if you can supply them, you will have every real estate agent eating out of your hand.

Whoever controls the customer controls the deal flow.

How Should You Approach Real Estate Agents?

If you are new to the business, you might have heard stories from other loan officers about how badly some agents treat loan officers. On the other hand, every real estate agent has heard stories of loan officers screwing up slam dunk loans and costing the agent a hefty commission. Both groups are taught to beware of the other. So how are we supposed to work together with all this animosity?

Partnership. In order to build strong, long lasting relationships with real estate agents, you need to approach and treat them as partners. Take an interest in them as people and in their business. Show them you can help them generate more business and make their lives more enjoyable. The average real estate agent, earning a decent income, works over 60 hours a week!

The relationship has to be WIN-WIN. It cannot be "Send me your buyers and I will do their loans". Nor can it be "Send me your buyers and I guarantee them the lowest rate". That is not what the realtor is looking for. Put yourself in his shoes. If you were an agent, what would you want from a lender?

Let's step into an agent's mind and see what he is thinking when we ask him to describe the perfect lender.

- Every loan program under the sun. No matter what kind of client I have or what he wants to buy, from vacant land to a mobile home to a three million dollar mansion, my lender should be able to do the loan.

- All credit ok. I don't want to lose prospects due to their credit. I know people with really bad credit pay more for loans, but I don't want to hear no from my lender.

- I want to be kept up to date on all buyers I send. I don't want to have to chase my lender down to see if the loan got approved or not. He should be proactive and let me know, via phone, fax, or email before I have to ask.

- My lender should not overcharge my clients. He doesn't have to be the cheapest of the cheap but he should be competitive. I understand he needs to make a living as well.

- He should have a pleasing personality and be easy to work with. When I send him a couple, I don't want to hear how rude he was or how he didn't seem to care about them, and that all he was concerned about was the origination fee. By sending him my buyers, he represents me. If he does something the buyers do not like, I look bad.

- He should provide me tools to make my job easier, like a way to pre-qualify potential buyers before I spend my time showing them properties. Either give me the software to do it myself, or make it available on his website. But I shouldn't have to call him every time I need a credit check.

- He should be loyal to me and send me leads whenever someone approaches him and says they want to buy or sell and do not have a realtor.

- He should do what he says he will. If he says he will get the paperwork to the title company on time, he should. I have enough things to worry about already without having to babysit a lender who isn't true to his word.

- My lender should behave in a totally ethical and moral way. Everything should be above board. I don't want to be dragged into any legal complications or law suits because my lender was a scam artist.

- I want to deal with a full time professional that has experience and will be in the business for a long time. I don't want to have to go around finding a new lender every couple years. I want a stable relationship with one person, not a faceless company, where I have to wait on hold every time I call.

- I want my lender to be an extension of me and my team. We should present a unified front to our customers.

If you can determine what an agent wants and needs, and find a way to give it to him, you have an excellent chance of getting his business and his loyalty.

COMMON PRACTICES FOR LOAN OFFICERS

How Do Most Loan Officers Get Real Estate Agents?

Method 1: Bribe Them

The most common advice given to loan officers is to go to the real estate offices and see if any agent needs help with a loan. Wholesale lender reps are told to do the same thing. They drop by unannounced and usually bring goodies for the loan officers in order to talk to them for a few minutes. The most common things loan officers bring agents are donuts and croissants in the morning, pizza and soda in the afternoon, and rate sheets. Lots and lots of rate sheets.

Method 2: Personal Correspondence

Letters and memos sent to agents. Getting their names and addresses is not very hard. Most states list all the names and addresses on their websites. Just go to your state's licensing website and you should be able to get a complete list of everyone with a real estate license. A better way is to get the names from their own advertising. Or you can just mail a letter to everyone in a certain office at the office address. Or you can get a list of every agent in the city if have you access to the MLS.

First you have to get your message read. If you send a letter in a sealed envelope, at least hand-address the envelope. Do not use address labels or your letter will never get opened. Once it is opened you have to convince the agent to read it and do what you want them to do—which is probably to call you.

Method 3: Seminars

Most real estate offices usually have an office meeting once a week. It is at these meetings the broker or manager goes over any new developments and offers some pep talk or marketing tidbits. If you can develop a short talk that can provide some benefit to the agents, the manager might let you speak. Some topics you can speak on are: credit scores, popular loan programs, down payment assistance, 100% loan programs, database management, marketing, and how interest rates work.

Keep in mind that you are not there to sell yourself. You are there to provide valuable information and to be an expert advisor that these agents can call whenever they need mortgage help. If all you talk about is how great you are and how cheap your rates are, no one will listen to you, and you will never be invited back. Give a good presentation to an office and you develop good will with all the agents in that office. If you are seen as an expert, chances are very good that you will be allowed to follow up with the agents, and that you will be approached by some of them if you talk about certain borrower types.

Method 4: Referrals

Most home sale transactions have at least one agent involved. Many have two—the listing agent and the selling agent. If a buyer comes to you and you do not know the buyer's agent, you need to do everything you can to get the buyer to recommend you to his agent. Make sure that loan goes smoothly, and ask the agent for more business.

Make sure you also contact the seller's agent. Introduce yourself as the lender and answer any questions they may have. But be careful not to give away any confidential information the buyers have shared with you. Keep the seller's agent in the loop during the loan to show your professionalism.

Tip: Ask the seller's agent if the sellers are staying in the neighborhood and if you can contact them regarding their loan. Most agents will agree. When the sellers see what a great job you are doing with the buyer's loan, they will be willing to listen to your sales presentation as well.

You can also ask people in your sphere of influence/database to introduce you to and recommend you to real estate agents they know or might have used in the past.

Should You Go After Buyer Agents Or Listing Agents?

All agents are the same right? Wrong! Agents specialize just like we do. The two main ways agents earn money is from selling a house and from helping people buy a house. All agents can do both. But some focus on one or the other. Most real estate trainers say that the money is in the listings. Meaning that once you get a homeowner to let you sell their house, you are free to let the other agents sell the house for you. And when it sells, you get a commission. On the other hand if you work with buyers, you have to spend time with each buyer and show them around until they buy. So a real estate agent can earn more money going after listings instead of buyers. The more listings you have the greater a chance of a commission. Plus, potential buyers will call you from the sign in the yard, and if they buy from you, you get a double commission.

So as a loan officer, you should focus on selling agents right? It depends. A listing agent has the potential to generate a lot of buyer leads. Everyone that calls a sign is a lead. And sign calls are one of the top ways all agents get business. The agent will have to have open houses to attract buyers. The agent will have to advertise the house resulting in more lead calls. And the sellers of the house will need to buy another house. If you work with a buyer's agent, she will have solid homebuyers, but fewer leads.

ADVANCED STRATEGIES

Create An Agent Info Pack

An agent info pack is some basic information about you and what you can do to help the agent. It should be given to any agent you want to do business with. It's like a business card with a lot of information. Your pack should have info on you, your company, your loan programs, USP, niche, why they should work with you, your guarantees, and lots and lots of testimonials.

You would give your pack to introduce yourself to any agent you work with or are referred to. So if you are doing a loan with a listing agent and a buyer's agent, send them each a pack. In it you could also detail what you will be doing, how you work, how they should contact you, and what your procedures are.

If you were referred to an agent from a friend, you should contact them first, and if they seem interested in talking to you further, send them a pack. Don't waste packs on agents who aren't courteous or considerate when you first talk to them. And don't send them to everyone on your agent mailing list, unless you have a lot of money.

Be #2

Let's be realistic. The majority of agents you contact will not work with you at first. And they will never work with you unless you follow up with them. Once you identify an agent you really want to work with, keep following up with that person until they either do business with you or die, whichever comes first. I have had loan officers in my coaching group that have followed up with certain agents for years before getting a chance to do a loan for them.

A great place to be is #2 in the agent's mind. If you are trying to get business from an agent who already works with one lender exclusively, you might want to try to get him to recommend you as a #2 lender to his buyers. Then you can show how you are better than lender #1.

And if you cannot do this, keep following up and stay in that agent's conscious mind by keeping your name in front of him. Eventually lender #1 is going to screw up and if you are #2, you have a great chance of moving into the #1 spot.

The Marketing To Real Estate Agents Toolkit is a great way to get past the initial hurdle of getting agents to meet with you and listen to what you have to say. I personally developed and tested the toolkit to make sure it works. And the results have been fabulous. Not a week goes by without at least one loan officer commenting on how the toolkit helped in getting realtor business.

Let me share with you how and why the toolkit works so even if you do not wish to purchase it, you can use it as a model to create your own system.

How Does The Marketing To Real Estate Agents Toolkit Work?

The toolkit gives you every tool you need to be able to:

1. Market to real estate agents in a professional way.

2. Get them to call you and have them want to meet with you.

3. Give them something they want that has real value.

4. Have a great meeting with them and impress them to the point where they want to work with you.

5. Follow up with the ones that don't send you business right away.

6. Make you stand out in the marketplace.

7. Get multiple leads and use the follow-up systems provided to convert a high percentage of these leads into loans that you can then take back to the real estate agent.

8. Generate referrals among real estate agents. Have one real estate agent tell his colleagues about how great you are.

HERE IS A SUMMARY OF THE SYSTEM:

- Offer something for free to get real estate agents to call you, so you can set up an interview.

- Meet with real estate agents and explain the benefits you provide, including a custom program that they desperately want to be able to use.

- Get business from real estate agents right away or follow up until you do.

First you get real estate agents to call you. Most loan officers break their backs trying to cold call agents asking for business. Or they go to their offices and hand out rate sheets and bribes (donuts or pizza). We do not want to do this. We want the agent to call us. This way, we are in control of the situation. We also are not pestering them, trying to beg for business. We appear more professional.

In order to get them to call us, I have created a special package that contains valuable information specifically for agents. We offer to give out these packages for free to any real estate agent who wants them. We use attention getting marketing concepts to attract their attention and pique their curiosity to the point where they have to call.

The package contains three special reports titled:

1. Real Estate Agents: How to Double Your Income in 90 Days

2. Agent Marketing on a Shoestring Budget: How to Jump-Start Your Business for Under $200

3. How to Instantly Increase Your Client's Credit Score

Included in our special package are these three special reports, information on our client follow-up system, information on our company, and an agent application.

In our ads, it says, "To get a free copy of your package just call our office". When they call, the receptionist explains that we would be happy to set a time so a representative can hand deliver the package and explain its contents.

After the meeting is scheduled, I meet with the real estate agent and use the script I prepared. At the end of the interview I present the package and ask if the agent would like to fill out an application to see if I will work with him. During the meeting I introduce our customer follow up program, which is a very valuable tool for any real estate agent. By explaining how it works and how it does not cost the agent anything, they want to work with me even more. If at that time they are still not ready to begin a business relationship, they go into the agent follow-up program until they are.

Working with real estate agents can make you a lot of money. But never compromise your values to work with one. Don't beg or appear desperate. If you have confidence in yourself and your abilities, that confidence will shine through and the agent will feel it.

CHAPTER **15**

"You've Got to Go See My Mortgage Guy, He's the Best Around."

What sparks a referral?

First, the definition. A referral is one satisfied customer telling a potential customer how happy he is with a business or transaction and that the potential customer should also go there.

Simple concept. It's been happening since hairy men hunted with fat bats.

Caveman Bob has a new club.

Caveman Bill says, "Ug,Ug, nice. Where you get?"

Caveman Bob: "John's Clubs and Other Blunt Objects in TarPits Mall."

Do you remember the last time you asked someone for a recommendation? Might have been for a restaurant or a doctor. Did you take the advice? Probably. Now think back to why you asked. If it was for a restaurant, you might have been in a new area and unfamiliar with your surroundings. You wanted to have a good time and be treated right. But you felt uneasy just walking into any place and taking your chances.

Bingo. That's exactly what happens with people looking for a mortgage. They have a vague idea of what they want (low rate, good service). But they have no clue who can provide it. They don't want to just walk into any office. Too risky. So they start doing research. They ask around. They find friends, relatives, anyone who has gone through the same experience. They gather opinions from those closest to them. Then they check out newspapers and the Internet.

People eventually find someone who has just gotten a mortgage and who says a zillion great things about his mortgage broker. Chances are these people will investigate this amazing mortgage broker. The broker automatically gets on the short list without doing anything. The previous customer did all the selling for him.

The phenomenon of the reticular activator comes into play here. Big words, simple concept. It's like an antenna rising from your head seeking information regarding what you are currently thinking about.

Example: You decide to buy a new car, a Mercedes convertible. As soon as you make this decision, your activator hunts for information about this car. And when you drive around, you notice Mercedes convertibles everywhere. You simply didn't notice them before. Your activator hunted them down.

The same thing happens to people in the home-buying market. Their activators scan for housing information. They automatically talk houses and mortgages with their friends. They "see" mortgage ads that they didn't notice before.

So basically referrals work two ways. A prospect can ask for a referral. Or while he is talking about the subject with someone, the other person can give the prospect a referral.

The second method works better. We want people to voluntarily talk about us—not be pushed into it.

People used to call this word of mouth. Nowadays it's called referral marketing. Whatever the name, it will last as long as people roam this planet. Make sure to master the techniques, and you will succeed in any business.

Referrals happen all the time. But to be successful we must cultivate them and not just wait for them. For true success, you must dictate how referrals come to you, when, and how many. Let's compare this to other forms of marketing. Direct mail brings returns of less than 2% on average. Newspaper and magazine ads have a lower return than that. Cold calling is against the law. Door knocking takes too long. Working with real estate agents works, but you are at the mercy of the agent for business.

People are simply bombarded by marketing. Everywhere you turn, someone is trying to get your money. Drive down the street and you will see more ads than traffic lights: on billboards, taxis, signs, even magnetic ones on cars. Competition is fierce, and not all the competition is honest and dependable. People get burned. Consumers feel they are not being treated properly.

More and more people feel they deserve to make money just because they show up to work, or open a business. Costs are going up for businesses while margins are going down. Customer service takes a back seat to profits.

This is all causing customers to be more aware, more careful of whom they do business with.

With that kind of consumer, it's tough to communicate, to get your sales message across. If you don't get through, how are they going to do business with you when they search for your service? Every business in America is asking that question right now. That includes the giants with billions in their ad budgets.

Relate this to the mortgage business. When consumers pick a tangible product, they can look at it and touch it before they buy. But mortgages are a service. How can the customer know from the beginning that we will do a good job and that we are not just out to make a fat check? There is no way for customers to know how good we are until after the fact. Even if we tell them, they will not believe us as much as they will believe someone they already trust.

So we need an edge. A better way to get through. And there is no better way than by referral. People like to do business with those they know, like, and trust. If they don't know you, a recommendation from a friend or family is the next best thing.

According to an online survey by Mortgage Originator Magazine, 57% of loan originators say the majority of their referrals come from past customers.

Referrals are your edge. They cut through the marketing clutter and put you on the short list of potential vendors. Or even in the No. 1 spot. Once there, the loan is yours to lose.

REFERRALS CLOSE AT A HIGHER RATE

Chris Faicco, a life insurance agent, did the following study. Of 5,640 qualified prospects, 2,240 were brought in by cold calling; 3,400 were brought in by referrals. From the cold-calling group they closed 56 sales, or 11.%. The referral group bought 452 times, or 40%! Even though 11% is nothing to laugh at, 40% is serious stuff. But I will tell you a secret right here: If you don't close 75% or more of all referrals you get, you are doing something wrong. Using the methods I will show you, you will get more referrals and they will be ready to do business with you when they show up.

THE BENEFITS OF REFERRALS

Why are referrals the way to go? Three main reasons:

1. Clients' attitude.

    I hate rate shoppers. Hate them with a passion. I have thrown people out of my office for just suggesting they can get a better rate somewhere else. And probably like you, I have been burned by people who, after I have locked their rate, go to another company because rates dropped an eighth of a percent.

    Even if they are not rate shoppers, if they come from any of our other advertising, most of the time in the initial meeting is spent on making them feel comfortable with me and my organization. I have to spend time talking about the way I differentiate myself from all the other brokers in my city. I have to tell them what they get from me that they don't get from anyone else. Basically I have to sell me, even before we talk about rates and fees.

And that is after we get them into the office. Just getting the appointment is a struggle. Unless they need a loan today, they don't want to come anywhere near an office because they are afraid they will get sold something.

I hate converting leads into prospects, too. Calling people I have never talked to, who knows what is going on in their life while I try to convince them they should meet with me? Yuck! Good thing I let my assistants handle most of that.

What I really enjoy is dealing with people who are open and honest about their situation—after they have made up their mind that they are getting their loan from me. When they make that decision, they change. Their attitude changes. Their guard goes down and they open up. They express their vulnerabilities and share their true wants and concerns. That is when I can best help them.

Which leads to people who have been referred. Talk about relaxing. When they call you, they sound conversational. They let you know that Joe told them to call you. They know that will get great service.

Referrals see you as a professional. They know that you can do the job right and you can get them a great deal just like you got their friends. That's why you were referred. Because of this shift in their perception of you, you spend less time convincing them that they should do business with you, that you are honest and capable. They already know that. So you can get down to business.

2. More money.

Referred customers are less likely to shop the rate. They might make sure you're not ripping them off. But if your rate is competitive, they will stay with you rather than risk a bad experience.

Think about it—why do people ask just what your rate is? That's because they have no other criteria to tell the difference between one mortgage company and another. We are all the same to most people. Money is a commodity, remember?

Play along with me. Let's say you need a plumber. You have a broken pipe in the wall. Not an emergency, but it needs to be fixed. If you don't have a regular plumber and can't get a recommendation from anyone, you look in the phone book. You call the first place listed, describe your problem, and ask when the firm can fix it and how much? You call the second place and ask the same thing. Now you have two numbers to compare. You call the third, then the fourth.

Most likely each plumbing place told you (a) how much it could cost or (b) they would have to come look at it first. Chances are none of the companies did anything to stand out. So you are left to make a decision based on price and the feeling you got from the person on the other end of the phone. That does not result in a very educated decision.

It is the same for customers when they are getting a loan. Is it any wonder that 70% of home buyers ask their realtor about what mortgage company to use?

Referred customers don't need to play this game. They can already tell you are different from any other mortgage company out there. You come recommended!

The bottom line: Per loan, you can make more money on a referred customer than a rate shopper.

Am I saying to charge more just because you can? No. I am saying that you are a professional in high demand and should be compensated accordingly. The best doctors can charge more per hour than regular doctors. And you don't have to worry as much about your customer running to another company after you've spent your time and money on him.

3. Least costly method of marketing.
Marketing can really cut into your funds. Ads, printing, postage, web pages, phone systems—they add up quickly. If you are tracking your marketing (you should track every ad you place), you know how much each lead costs. Mortgage companies can spend $200–$300 per qualified lead through their own marketing efforts.

Referrals do not cost nearly as much. You need to spend money to facilitate referrals, but that costs a fraction of what a normal marketing campaign goes for. If you can get your per lead cost down from $200 to $20, that's an extra $180 per lead in your pocket!

BEING REFERABLE

In order for someone to recommend you, certain things must already be in place.

1. The referrer must know you, like you, and trust you.

2. The referrer must believe you give excellent service so that his own reputation will be upheld.

3. The referrer must remember you and think about you often.

4. The referrer must know how to get into contact with you.

5. The referred must know that you want and appreciate referrals.

If you are missing any of those five criteria, you are missing out on a boatload of referrals.

In order to have continuous referrals your goals must be to:

- Turn suspects into prospects.

- Turn prospects into customers.

- Turn customers into clients.

- Turn clients into friends.

Friends buy, refer, and make business fun.

HOW TO GENERATE REFERRALS

The first and easiest way to generate referrals is to mine your database. Extract the hidden gold.

If you provide Amazing Service™ to your clients, you will get referrals automatically. Not many, but a few. It is up to you to implement a system to generate more. Again, the referral is the best type of loan you can get. It's no wonder most top producers work only on a referral basis.

You, too, might want to work that way. No more marketing, prospecting, cold calling, or dealing with rate shoppers. You work only with people who have been sent to you by someone in your database. So make sure to do everything you can to build your database as quickly as possible. It is truly the holy grail of referrals.

Now comes the interesting part.

In order to generate referrals, you must do one thing: ASK.

Then you ask again and again and again—for as long as you are in business.

When I was getting my training to be a realtor (which I am not anymore), I enrolled in an expensive training class that was supposed to help my business. The main marketing vehicle taught was cold calling.

According to the trainer, the best way to get customers was to call people and ask, "Hello, Mr. Doe, I am Ameen with XYZ Properties. I was calling to see if you knew anyone who would be interested in buying or selling a house."

After 100 calls, someone would say something like, "Yeah, I think I want to move. Can you give me more information?"

What I was actually asking for was a referral. But even after thousands of calls, NO ONE gave a referral. The real estate trainer knew this was going to happen as well. The reason they said to use this line was to get the homeowner's guard down. Homeowner's don't typically tell strangers they are thinking of moving. But if you ask them if the know someone else, they might continue to talk to you.

Why do you think this method of asking for referrals didn't work?

Because the homeowner didn't know the caller, much less trust him. This is the perfect way NOT to ask for a referral.

Another technique commonly used is this: "Oh, by the way, do you know anyone looking to buy or refinance a house?" That's not the way to ask either. Getting referral business is not an afterthought. It is not something you do on the way out of the house or while hanging up. It is serious business—yours. Take time to give it the respect it deserves. It deserves its own system that you can use again and again effectively.

And by asking a yes or no question, you are setting yourself up to hear a no. When put on the spot, people feel uncomfortable. Unless you set the scene to ask for the referral, it will be unexpected. For the customer, the easiest way to get out of that situation, and the first thing that comes to their mind, is "No."

Joe Gandolfo writes in his book *Sell and Grow Rich* about his conversation with a paint salesman. While in the salesman's place of business, Joe saw plaques and trophies all over the place. Here's their banter:

JG: What are all these plaques and trophies for?

Paint Salesman: I won them for being the top paint sales-man in the United States.

JG: How did you become number one?

PS: Because I know the magic words.

JG: What magic words?

PS: I say, "I need your help." When you ask for help, no one ever says no.

JG: What help do you ask for?

PS: I ask for the names of three friends.

STEP BY STEP

Here is a process to ask for and generate referrals.

Step 1: Every time you deal with clients or prospects—in person, on the phone, email, or letter—ask for a referral. But before you do, make them want to give you a referral.

Tell them you enjoy doing business with them and people who have a similar sense of values and ethics. Tell them you want to work with their acquaintances and that you are willing to offer them the chance to refer their friends and family to you.

Help them see a referral in their mind. Help them understand who out of all their family and friends would most likely benefit from your service. Tell them what the person might be doing right now or talking about. Then show how they would benefit from your service.

Step 2: Tell clients that you will help friends and family by consulting with them about their situation. Explain that this will not be a sales call or presentation, but just a fact-finding mission to see if they need help with anything.

Do this with every person you come in contact with, and your referrals will skyrocket.

Step 3: Systemize it. After learning how to ask, you need to create a system in your business that does the work for you. Everything you do should be systemized, and generating referrals is no different.

Here is a simple system you can use:

1. Make sure you provide Amazing Service™—deliver what you promise.

2. Take pride in your work and yourself.

3. Differentiate yourself from your competition.

4. Show interest in your clients by asking them about themselves.

5. Do something for the customer before you ask for a referral. This will induce the law of reciprocity.

6. Ask for the referral when the customer is most receptive. This will usually be after filling out the 1003, getting approved, and at closing.

7. Give the customer logical and emotional reasons why he should refer someone to you.

8. Offer to give the referral a discount or freebie.

9. Have the person call or contact the referral himself.

10. Reward the person for giving you a referral to encourage more in the future. Be careful to watch out for RESPA.

11. Keep in contact with people who have sent you referrals. I suggest you do this via a monthly newsletter. A great source for mortgage newsletters is FreeMortgageNewsletters.com.

This system outlines the basics. Several chapters could be written on each one of these steps. In fact, we have. The material above has been taken from one of our products called *Referrals on Demand*. This system is the most comprehensive and result-oriented referral marketing system in the market today.

This chapter covers just the surface of generating referrals. Because they are so crucial to having a great business, I encourage you to get *Referrals on Demand* to complete your education about referrals. In it, I don't just talk about asking; I give you the actual scripts to use. I show you dozens of ways to reward your customers for referrals without violating RESPA. I show you how to provide Amazing Service™ that is so far above and beyond what other mortgages companies do that customers will go out of their way to talk about you. And I show you how to get people in your database to want to talk to their friends about you—converting them into your own personal sales force.

SECTION 4
MAKE 'EM SAY YES.

So now that you have the leads flowing in, what do you do
with them? Turn them into loans.

Easier said than done.

The difficulty of this process is determined by the source of
your lead. If the lead is a referral, you job is much easier. If the
lead is a bought lead and has had four loan officers call already,
your job will be much, much tougher.

The average prospect is hesitant to trust any salesperson.
And as loan officers, that is what we are—we sell loans. As
such, we have to overcome this initial reluctance and get the
prospect to trust us. There are hundreds of books on different
selling techniques, including trust based selling. And there are
ten times more on closing techniques.

This section has been written to show you how to get the
prospect to think the way you want him/her to. By influencing

the prospect we can get him/her to do what we wish more often than not.

This is not to say you will be able to convert 100% of your leads. No one is that good. So you must be ready for rejection as well. In the end, it is a numbers game. The more leads, the more loans.

Generate enough leads and even with lousy service, predatory pricing, and no market knowledge you can still make a living. But if you offer fair rates, Amazing Service™, and are a mortgage master, you can make a killing with just a few leads.

The chapters in this section will help you get the prospect on your side. But you still must do all that you learned in previous chapters. Your job becomes easier if you are seen as the expert in your field. It is easier if the person already likes you because they have something in common with you. If the person is part of your niche, he/she will feel that you are specially suited to help him/her. A referral from a realtor or someone in your database is the easiest prospect to convert into a loan because most of the selling has already been done for you.

Here's a marketing secret: Just about everything we buy, we buy for emotional reasons. Before you start arguing with me, think about it a second. Why do people buy Mercedes Benz? To look rich, to feel good about themselves, and to be envied. But if you ask a Mercedes owner why she bought it, she will tell you it was because of the safety features or the quality of the car. Does anyone need to spend $60k on a car when a $20k car will do just as well? All it does is take you from one place to another.

People buy using emotion. Then back up their choice using logic. Not the other way around. And psychologists and marketing experts have proven this. One psychologist even went as far as to say that a prospect will decide within three seconds to do business with you or not. I don't know if I buy that one, but emotions are very powerful. And this section is here to teach you how to get your prospect's emotions in line with yours.

HOW TO GET ANYONE
TO DO WHAT YOU WANT

As a loan officer, your job is to get loan apps. Lots of leads make that job easier.

But it doesn't end there. You still must convert leads into applications. That's where the initial interview or appointment comes in. Prospects decide whether to use you based on what their subconscious feels about you. You might be great, but that's only part of the equation. If the prospect gets a negative vibe from you, it's over.

This chapter deals with the Laws of Influence. You see, our brains work in mysterious ways. Scientists know that most of the time, what we do makes no sense. Thanks to psychologists, we grasp some of why we do what we do. Many of our actions are controlled by the subconscious mind.

Every day our brain has to perform billions of actions. Every time we move, several muscles churn. Every time we hear something, the brain performs thousands of functions to understand, catalog, and respond to the noise. There is no way we can consciously think about every decision we make before we act.

Take driving. When you first drove a car you had to pay attention to every detail. After years of driving, you can do it while eating, talking on the phone, and singing along with the radio. The actions involved with driving can now be done by the subconscious mind. We don't have to think about them anymore.

We can use the same phenomena to our advantage as loan originators. This chapter aims to outline the most powerful Laws of Persuasion so we all can make more money.

Keep in mind a simple rule of persuasion: **It is easier to get people to do something if they like you.** The more similar you are to your prospects, the more they will affiliate with you and are more likely to agree to any request.

THE FIRST AND MOST COMMON IS THE LAW OF RECIPROCITY

This law simply says that when people do something for you, you want to do something to repay them. In a sense, you feel you "owe" them until you pay back their favor. If someone buys you a birthday gift, you are obligated to buy them one in return—even if you don't like them and didn't want a gift from them in the first place.

How Others Use This

We can use the Law of Reciprocity in our business just like the Hare Krishnas do. Robert Cialdini author of *The Psychology of Influence* observed that Hare Krishnas draw money from just about everyone they come into contact with even though most of the public is not into Hare Krishnas. The Hares counter that negative attitude by giving people gifts—books, magazines, flowers. Even if the marks try to return the items, the Hare Krishnas say, "No, it is our gift to you." Only then are marks asked to contribute. After receiving a gift, most people give something.

According to the Disabled American Veterans, their usual 18% donation response *nearly doubled* when the same mailing request included a small free gift.

How We Can Use It

The best thing to give for free is information. If you take time to explain the mortgage process, applicants will likely feel indebted to you. Recently I shopped for a high-definition TV for my bedroom. I visited several stores and websites. But I couldn't pull the trigger. I simply didn't want to buy the wrong TV. Then my wife and I stopped at Tweeter, a home entertainment store. The salesman asked general questions. When he found that I didn't know much about HDTV, he tried to explain it. After twenty minutes and several demonstrations, I finally understood.

That was a healthy exercise. No one in any other store had bothered to explain what I needed, what the differences were, and what my options were. This man invested time to inform me. I did not buy anything that day, but when I do buy, I will only buy from him. Even if it costs more than at any other store.

Here's how it works at my company: When someone shows up for an appointment, we bring him a drink. A can of soda or a bottle of water. Even if he refuses, we still give it to him or bring something else to drink. All during the interview, that drink sits there in front of him as a reminder that I did something nice for him.

Before the interview even starts, we give the potential clients a free book. A real bookstore book. We buy such books from a remainder book wholesaler. They cost $2 or $3 each. We present the book as an unannounced gift for stopping in. Everyone takes the book. And it doesn't matter what the book is about. We try to collect titles, by popular nonfiction authors, that appeal to everyone.

By providing something for free, even if it is not expensive, we can assume that we will receive something in return. In our case, we want the loan. People have a hard time saying no when you've been nice to them. The trick is not to let your donor return your gift. Be careful, though. If the customer suspects you are trying to bribe or trick him, the technique will backfire.

Another way to induce reciprocity is take someone to lunch. This is a cost-effective way to generate business—especially with a real estate agent. If the agent gives you even one loan, you have paid for the meal 100 times. Plus you have an opportunity to develop a friendship that could pay dividends for years to come.

Here's an exercise: Come up with ten ways you can induce reciprocity from a prospective client or referral partner. What can you give that will make him want to return the favor? Remember, the cost is irrelevant. It's the gesture that counts. Even if the customer doesn't like you, you can get him to do what you want through reciprocity.

Another aspect of the law says the gift can be much smaller than the favor later requested. So a book can and does turn into a loan.

What if you go through the motions and the prospect still does not agree to get the loan from you? You can suggest an alternate method of compensation—like the names of friends who might need a loan. Or an introduction to his real estate agent. Many individuals who do not like to give out names of friends do so in this fashion.

The Law of Dissonance

This law says people will naturally act in a manner that is consistent with their cognitions (beliefs, attitudes, and values). We want our beliefs, values, and actions to be aligned. When they are not, we feel dissonance, that uneasy feeling in our gut. The further we get from alignment, the more dissonance we feel, until we snap. When we can't take it anymore, we have to physically realign ourselves.

Some of the ways we reduce the dissonance we feel is through:

Denial: What problem?

Modification: Changing our thinking to agree with our actions.

Reframing: Looking at the situation in a different light. "It wasn't important to me anyway."

Rationalization: Justifying our behavior and changing our expectations.

Buyer's Remorse is a form of cognitive dissonance. That is why many states have three-day right of rescissions on refinance loans. Some people just cannot make up their minds;

when they do, they feel bad about it. They feel dissonance—that perhaps they made a wrong decision.

In one study, people were interviewed while in line to place a bet at a racetrack and questioned again after they placed the bet. They were much more confident with their decision after they had already placed their bet. They had the same information. The only difference was they had now publicly declared what their decision was, and they had to believe in it.

This is crucial to remember: Most people try to follow through when they promise they will do something—especially when it is in writing. Small commitments can lead to larger ones down the road. First you have to get your foot in the door. Public commitments are stronger than private ones.

How This Has Been Used

Social psychologist Steven Sherman called a sample of residents and asked them what their response would be if they were asked to volunteer three hours to collect contributions for the American Cancer Society. He didn't ask them to volunteer, he only wanted to know what their answer would be if someone did ask them. Many of them agreed because they did not want to seem uncharitable. When the Cancer Society called a few days later to really ask for help, there was a 700% increase in people agreeing to volunteer.

Toy companies use this method every Christmas. There is always a must-have toy that every child wants. Parents promise to get that exact toy. But what happens? A frenzy for that toy and a shortage. The toy companies don't make enough, and most children get something else for Christmas. Then in January, this toy miraculously pops up in stores. The parents who promised to get this toy are back in stores buying it—only because they made a promise. Manufacturers have been using this ploy for years, and people still go along with it!

How We Can Use This

Many loan officers have a problem with people filling out loan apps, then getting their loan somewhere else. Either the rate drops, another company slashes its origination fee to do the loan, or someone says bad things about you and the applicant feels dissonance in doing business with you. Here is what you can do to limit this behavior.

1. Before you do any work, get money upfront for appraisal and credit report. If someone is not serious, he will balk and leave, saving you a lot of time. If he is serious, he will have no problem putting up a small amount of money that needs to be spent anyway.

2. Have the applicant fill out the application in her own handwriting. Yes, it will take longer. But when someone agrees to something, and she puts it in writing, she is much more likely to go through with it. She will feel dissonance if she doesn't. This is why companies have contests for people to write about their products. The firms don't care how well you write. All they want is for you to make a written endorsement of their products. Then it will be tough for you to switch brands.

3. Get a loan applicant to rate you and your service (in writing) if she didn't fill out an application at the first interview. Follow up by mail a couple of days later with the person's comments. "You said this and this," and include a copy of what the person wrote.

The real way to stop having loans fall out or losing them to other companies is to pre-sell prospects before they come in to meet you.

USE THE FOOT-IN-THE-DOOR TECHNIQUE

If you can get someone to grant you a small request, it's easier to get him to agree to a large request. Salespeople use the technique by asking for "five minutes of your time" and even a free demonstration.

Here's how it works: In 1966, psychologists Jonathan Freedman and Scott Fraser sent a researcher acting as a volunteer to a California neighborhood asking homeowners if they would put a "Drive Carefully" billboard in their front lawn. The researcher then showed a picture of the sign obstructing the view of a beautiful house. Most people refused to put up the sign. But in one group, 76% of them agreed. The difference was that two weeks earlier, these people had been asked by a different volunteer to sign a petition that favored "keeping California beautiful." Almost everyone agreed to the small request and most then agreed to the large request only because they had already agreed to something previously with a similar message. They had already committed.

To use dissonance, get prospects to commit. Try to get their commitment in writing and in front of a few people. Car salesmen do this by getting us to sign several documents or initialing the price we would pay for the car even before the final negotiations take place.

Use questions in your interview that require yes answers. Sales trainers tell us the best way to close a presentation is with six "yes" questions. Every time prospects agree with you, it's that much easier for them to agree with your plan.

Start with a small request. Get them to agree to let you send them information. Get them to agree to join your mailing list. If they don't agree, create dissonance. "You don't want rates to go up, do you?" Show them they are not keeping their commitment. "I thought you were serious about buying a home." "You agreed with the fees before, so now why do you need to think it over?"

Then there's a third step: Offer them a solution, a way out. Of course, the solution is to get their loan from you. Offer your service in a way that makes it easy for them to agree.

THE LAW OF CONNECTIVITY

This law says the more we feel connected to, liked by, and attracted to someone, the more persuasive that person becomes. Four main factors are involved: attraction, similarity, people skills, and rapport.

Yes, your clothes determine how successful you will be in originating. You must dress like whomever you are targeting. It's part of getting closer. Show an interest in the person. Bond with her by using the person's name in the conversation. Research shows that if you use a person's first name at the beginning and end of a sentence, your chance of persuasion increases. Also smile a lot and show respect.

Touching the person slightly can make a huge difference.

The first few seconds of a loan interview will often make or break the application. If the prospect gets a negative feel from you, she will not do the loan with you no matter what you offer.

How We Can Use This

By smiling, using the person's name, touching her on the hand or shoulder, and paying attention to what she has to say, you have a greater chance of getting someone to do what you want.

If you are attractive, you should use your good fortune. Sex does sell. You don't have to dress provocatively. But showing people that you are an attractive person will only help you. And when we come in contact with a person of the opposite sex, looks play an even larger role. Studies show that attractive females can persuade men more easily than unattractive ones. And attractive males can persuade females more easily then unattractive males.

It's called the Halo Effect. We view attractive people in a more positive way. Because we view them as positive, we want to be like them, and for them to like us. So what do you do if you are not the Madison Avenue picture of beauty? Don't give up. I'm no Brad Pitt, and I'm still doing pretty well. Here's what else you can do:

- Dress nicely and professionally at work.

- Keep up your hygiene. For some reason people do not trust men with beards. So if you have one, you might want to lose it.

- Be in shape. A small waist is a big factor in drawing positive responses.

- Look successful. People want to do business with successful people. So fix your office accordingly. And drive a high-end, clean car.

- Be an expert. Show that you are worth it. Display your awards, certificates, and degrees so prospects can be awed.

- Master the art of communication. A strong orator can make his case even if he is not that good-looking. Join Toastmasters if you fear speaking in public or want to improve.

- Work on your nonverbal communication. Get a book in the library about this and study it. 50% to 80% of communication is nonverbal.

- Use other laws of persuasion such as social validation by posting testimonials all over the place.

- Have your interview process and script memorized. Don't wing it; there is too much at stake.

THE LAW OF SOCIAL VALIDATION

This law suggests that we feel good when we see others doing what we want to do, and look to others for help in deciding what we should do. If we do not know how to act in a new situation, we look around to get clues from others.

There was a famous test in New York City, where from between one to fifteen people stared up at the sky. The more people that were doing it, the more people stopped what they were doing, came over, and looked up. Soon there was a whole mob.

HOW OTHERS USE THIS

On televised fundraisers, the people manning the phones are instructed to pretend they are talking on the phone when the camera turns their way to make it seem like the place is inundated with calls.

HOW WE CAN USE THIS

Everyone wants to do business with successful people. No one wants to do business with the guy desperate for the business. We all believe that if a company is busy, it must be good. You've experienced this while shopping for a restaurant. When you see the parking lot is empty, you pass it. Restaurants know this trick. So they park their own cars in front to make it look like the place is jumping.

By showing social proof, you are validating that others like you. The best way to do this is through testimonials. You MUST have testimonials. A written compliment from a cus tomer glitters with gold. It's that valuable. A few testimonials sprinkled in your interviews will turn more prospects into applications.

Prospects are scared. They are overwhelmed. They might have talked to five people already about mortgages, and everyone said something different. Your job is to put them at ease. At some point you must say great things about yourself. It's part of the sales pitch.

What really helps is when someone else says good things about you. That carries more weight. And the more testimonials you have, the better. If you have ten testimonials praising your after-hour service, prospects will feel relieved if that is their concern. If they are worried about the rate, display testimonials concerning your low rate.

Present your testimonials in a book and leave it in the waiting room. Add an endorsement at the bottom of your letterhead. Use all of them on your website. Add them to direct mail and marketing brochures. Put a good one on your business card. Frame them and hang them in your office. The more the better.

But what if you don't have any? Use pictures. Take photos of you and your friends. Take pictures with past clients in front of their homes. Then post these pictures all over your office. Create a "Wall of Happy Clients" with pictures of everyone smiling.

When you have a closing, send postcards to homes in that neighborhood. Realtors do this with great success. When someone moves to the neighborhood, they send a postcard to twenty houses up and down that street introducing the new family and their services.

You know what makes an impression? A pile of files in your office. When someone visits the office, refer to it. "Sorry I couldn't meet with you earlier. As you can see from this stack, I have so many loans in process that I have a very tight schedule." They don't have to be loan files. In fact, if you keep loan files lying around, you might be violating a particular mortgage law. The image we want to portray is that you are busy.

THE LAW OF SCARCITY

This law sits in the middle of the persuasive process. In a nutshell, it says opportunities are more exciting when they are less available. This is why gold and diamonds command top dollar. People think they are valuable because they are scarce.

Another angle to this law: People shift into action when they're afraid of losing something. We do not like restrictions or missing out on anything. This law applies even when people aren't that interested in an item or goal.

Ever hear of Romeo and Juliet? What are the chances that such youngsters (13 and 15) would fall in love so deeply that they would kill themselves? Not that good, until you add in the fact that this love was forbidden by both sets of parents. If the parents had not objected so strongly, the relationship probably wouldn't have lasted more than a few weeks.

HOW OTHERS USE THIS

The Beanie Baby craze came on when the manufacturer "retired" certain animals. This caused prices to soar and people to pile into stores. It is the same thing with any collectible. Certain coins are worth more because they were mistakes.

Stores use this law to create shopping frenzies. They use one item as the bait. They place it at a low price, but make only a few available. When they finally open the doors, people rush in to grab as many as they can. Another phenomenon: Shoppers grab things around this item as well. And these products go for big bucks.

A beef importing company ran the following test. The staff was instructed to call customers and ask them to purchase beef in one of three ways. One group got the normal pitch. The second group got the normal pitch, plus evidence that imported beef was going to be in short supply in coming months. The third group got the normal pitch and were told beef will be in short supply, but that this information would not be available to the public.

The second group bought twice as much as the first group. The third group bought SIX times as much as the first group.

HOW WE CAN USE THIS

You must be in HIGH demand. You must play hard to get—even if you are starving and need a loan to pay for your newborn's milk. As the saying goes, don't let 'em see you sweat. Clients want to work with successful people.

I emphasize exactly that In The Marketing To Real Estate Agents Toolkit. To get a realtor to work with you, you must create an atmosphere that you do not need his business. The trick is to make him think he needs you more than you need him.

If I call my attorney and she picks up the phone herself, I know she is not busy. That is not the attorney I want if I am going to court.

If you have someone handling your phone, have him follow this script: "Mr./Ms. Loan Officer is with a client right now. Let me see if he/she can take your call."

Use a similar message for your cell phone: "Hello. If you are calling during business hours, I am probably with a client. Please leave your name and number, and I will get back to you."

The more you stress that you are busy and have other clients, the more your clients and prospects will feel that you are the one to work with.

Also, make sure you work by appointment only. If a prospect calls and wants you to come over right away, and you allow them to, you just lost a lot of points. Say instead, "Sorry. I have other clients who have scheduled appointments. When would you like to schedule yours?" Even if you have no one else scheduled. It is all about perception. Prospects must perceive you as in demand.

THE LAW OF WORDS

This law says that words have a huge impact on results.

If you were selling a product, which of these three phrases do you think will sell the most?

- Half-price

- Buy one, get one free

- 50% off

They all mean the same thing. But the second phrase out-sells the others by close to 40%!

If you want someone to do something and you say, "Can you please do this?" you will get less cooperation than if you say, "Let's do this." or "Why don't we do this?".

When you want people on your side, use words that create vivid mental pictures. Attorney Gerry Spence said, "Don't say he suffered pain. Tell me what it felt like to have a broken leg with the bone sticking out through the flesh. Tell me how it was! Make me see it! Make me feel it!"

Know when to stop talking. Every good negotiator knows that silence is golden. After you make a request, be silent. Let the other person respond. Even if he takes a long time. Do not budge until you get a response. Then you can continue negotiating.

HOW OTHERS USE THIS

People are trained to comply. So if we repeatedly ask for what we want, we are more than likely to receive it.

A researcher approached people lined up at a copy machine. When she said, "Excuse me, I only have five pages. May I use the copy machine because I am in a rush?" 94% of people let her cut in line. When she said, "Excuse me, I have five pages. May I use the copy machine?" 60% let her in. And when she said, "Excuse me, I have five pages. May I use the copy machine because I have to make some copies?" 93% complied.

The reason she wanted to cut in line had no effect on the answer she got. But by adding the word "because," she was able to get 33% more compliance.

How We Can Use This

1. Add a reason to why you are asking.

2. Make the reason paint a picture in the mind of the client.

3. Use everyday language when asking.

4. Keep your sentences short.

5. Use words—such as "you," "we," "us"—that will cause the prospect to feel that the two of you are already working as a team.

6. Don't use words that portray a negative image. Instead of asking someone to pay an application fee, you can ask for a reservation deposit, to make sure you will set aside the time to work personally on his file.

7. Don't use too much jargon. Hardly anyone outside our business knows what a 1003 is.

The Law Of Contrast

Create extra value by comparing two or more items. This law is based on our perception of items or events that happen right after the other. Contrasting two alternatives can distort or amplify our perception.

You can try this one at home. Fill three buckets with water—one with hot water, one with cold, and another at room temperature. Simultaneously, put one hand in the hot water and the other hand in the cold water. Leave them there for 30 seconds. Now put both hands into the room temp water. The results are shocking. The hand that was in the hot bucket is going to feel cold, and the hand that was in cold water will feel hot. Even though the water is not cold or hot.

So yes, when you are in a meeting don't present after someone who just made a great presentation. Always go after a lousy presentation.

Use the Gingsu Knife method: This is where salespeople show you what you are going to get and the price, then they add something else, then something else, then something else. They keep adding free bonuses until the price seems so small, you almost have to order.

Reduce it to the ridiculous: If a prospect balks at your fees and complains, figure out what your fees are costing over the life of the loan—$5,000 in fees is only $167 a year over 30 years. Compare that with the thousands of dollars you will be saving them in interest.

Shift the focus: Two groups were given the same burgers. One group was told the burgers were 75% lean. The other group was told the burgers were 25% fat. The first group rated the burgers of higher quality and taste. The second group rated the burgers as fatty, greasy, and low quality.

The University of Colorado wanted to keep students off the campus grass. Signs that said "Don't Walk on the Grass" didn't work. So administrators tried signs that said "Give Earth a Chance." Like magic, people kept off the grass.

Big, then small: First make a large, unreasonable demand that will likely be refused, then follow with a smaller proposal. People accept the second request more readily than if they were asked only the second request. The smaller request seems like a concession on your part.

A girl who sold the most Girl Scout cookies one year was on the *Tonight Show*. When asked how she sold so many cookies, she did her pitch. She would go up to people and ask, "Sir, can you please make a $1,000 donation to the Girl Scouts?" Once they said no, she said, "Well then, how about buying a few boxes of cookies instead?" This technique sold thousands of boxes.

How Others Use This

Real estate agents use this when they show homes. The first few properties are called set-up properties. These are over-priced dumps. Then the agent shows the property she thinks the buyers will like. They like it more because they compare it to the dumps they just saw.

Look at Before and After pictures in diet commercials. The person is down and depressed in the Before picture, but upbeat, smiling, with erect posture, and a tan in the After picture.

When charity solicitors call for a donation, they begin by asking you how you are. Usually you reply, "Fine" or "Doing well." The solicitor proceeds to say, "I'm glad you're doing so well. I'm calling to see if you would like to make a donation to help the unfortunate victims of ..."

In one study, 18% of people donated without the initial "How are you doing this evening" while 32% donated after the greeting.

HOW WE CAN USE THIS

Start high. Use that Girl Scout cookie method. State outrageous fees, then cross them out and list your real fees. Make sure to make the second request right after you get the answer to the first. Timing is important. I saw this done brilliantly in a seminar. The speaker talked about his program until everyone wanted it. Then he wrote the price: 1895. Everyone was shocked. After he was sure everyone saw it, he drew an S on top of the one. So it became $895. Everyone was relieved. Suddenly $895 felt much smaller and more affordable.

When you talk about your fees or services, compare apples to oranges. "1% Origination is not for doing the loan. It is for the decades of my experience, the full staff of people working on your behalf to make sure your loan goes through without a hitch. It is for peace of mind that you will not lose the house of your dreams because of a simple error on our part. It is for the 24 different activities that we do to make sure you get the lowest rates possible. It is for the ability to search 248 lenders for the best program and loan terms that apply only to you. It is for an invitation to my once-a-year Customer Appreciation Gala."

If you are still having trouble justifying your fees, show customers what you do. Create a list of all the jobs you or your company must perform to make sure the loan goes through. Type up this list, laminate it, and keep it by your desk. Then show it in all your interviews with prospects and say, "I know the loan fees can sometimes seem excessive, but here is what I am going to do to earn my fees." Go over a few points on the list. Don't let them leave with the list. You don't want them taking it to another loan officer, who can just say, "Yeah, everybody does those things."

Another trick is to get the GFE and make sure the prospects know what all the expenses are. Make sure to say that it is no use to shop those fees because they will be the same everywhere.

Guarantee your work. That will convert more into applications. Whether it be a rate or a service guarantee, put it in writing and show it to prospects.

If you have a prospect who says another company is offering a lower rate, and you know that rate is a lowball, ask the prospect to get that rate guaranteed by the other company. Ask if that firm will guarantee that rate in writing. It won't, and that will put more doubt in the prospect's mind.

THE LAW OF EXPECTATIONS

People make decisions based on how others expect them to perform. They fulfill those expectations whether they are negative or positive. Surprisingly, these expectations have a greater influence on strangers than on those we know and trust. Don't believe me? Here are some examples.

Among prison inmates, 90% were told by their parents while growing up, "They're going to put you in jail."

Many schools have Dress-Up Day, like on Halloween. One school had Grubby Day. The school received more complaints about student behavior on this day than any other day of the year. Dress codes set up expectations.

When a principal and the custodian told a grade school class how clean and neat its room was, the amount of litter on the floor the following few days was less than half the normal amount.

When small children hurt themselves, they look to their parents for info. If a mother runs over to her child and shows concern, the child cries. If the parent laughs, the child also laughs.

We can also call this law the Placebo Effect. The same principles apply.

How Others Use This

In marketing, I have learned that you get more people to do what you want when you tell them exactly what you want them to do in detail. All of my advertising has the words Order Now or Call Me Right Now, at the bottom. Why? Because my tests have shown that without these words, fewer people order/call. By telling them exactly what I want them to do, or what I expect them to do, they do it more often.

How We Can Use This

When you sell, expect the person to comply. Salespeople are told to assume the sale. You must do the same. Why wouldn't a prospect want to do business with you? They would be crazy not to. So don't ask. Assume. "Initial these pages, and we can get started" is better than "Please sign the application."

If prospects are still hesitant, ask them why. Make sure to go over some possible reasons first.

"Mr. Prospect, it seems you are still uncertain. Let me see if I can alleviate your fears. There is no one else who can offer you a better rate. I have 278 lenders, while the average mortgage company uses only six. I offer 1,084 loan programs, so I have what you need. I am wiling to put myself and my team to work on your loan to accomplish the 24 different objectives we have for your loan. No other mortgage company will put what it does in writing. I offer you a guarantee in writing that my rate and service cannot be beat. I will send you on a seven-night cruise if can you prove me wrong.

"There is no logical reason that I can think of why you shouldn't move forward today. In fact, rates could go up and you might lose money if you wait. Now what is it that is holding you back?"

That script is powerful. Notice I use specifics: 278 lenders is more convincing than over 100. 1,084 loan programs is better than dozens.

THE LAW OF INVOLVEMENT

This law says that the more you engage someone's five senses, and involve him mentally and physically, the easier it is to persuade him.

When people were told to "imagine how cable TV will provide you broader entertainment," 47% bought a subscription compared with 20% who bought without that one line.

Use words that require a "yes" answer.

If you used these techniques, isn't it likely that you will be able to make more money? You have noticed how some of these techniques have been used on you in the past, haven't you? Isn't it your responsibility to learn all you can about marketing? Don't you think you should give 110% to getting your business off the ground by using all the techniques taught in this book?

How Others Use This

One of the best ways to take advantage of this law is to get the customer to fill out the order form by himself. Cancellations are much lower when the customer fills out everything in his own handwriting.

How We Can Use This

Use image-laden words to describe the services you perform and the desired result.

"Hassle-free" is a good term, but "never lift a finger" is better. Best is "all you have to do is sign here, then show up at closing."

When you negotiate with the "cutthroat" lenders, make sure the borrowers know this. As well as when you do battle with the unrelenting underwriting trolls.

Referrals are a great way to get people to buy into you. Once people refer you, they are stuck to you. It would be inconsistent with the image of themselves if they sent people to you, then used a different mortgage company themselves.

Create a competition. Offer a nice prize and tell people in your database to enter. Get them to tell their homeowner friends to enter as well. That way you get cheap advertising, you get referrals (your clients will tell them that "their" mortgage company is having a contest), and you get new names to add to your database.

Use repetition. Stay in touch with your database on a monthly basis at least. You need to stay in their face, in their conscious mind.

Use proper questions. The structure of the question will determine the response. Take an interview concerning a basketball player. When people were asked "How short is he?" they answered 69 inches. When asked "How tall is he?" they answered 79 inches.

Other examples:

"How much more is the other company charging you?" "How much am I saving you per month?"

"How cheap do you want my fees to be?" "Here is my value-driven cost structure."

Good persuaders don't take "no" for an answer. According to Calvin Coolidge, "Successful people always have high levels of persistence and don't give up until they have reached their objective. Nothing in the world can take the place of persistence. Talent will not. Nothing is more common that unsuccessful men with talent. Genius will not. Unprepared genius is almost a proverb. Education will not. The world is full of educated derelicts. Persistence, determination, and hard work make the difference."

THE LAW OF ASSOCIATION

To maintain order, our brains link things together. Experiences are linked with emotions, feelings, memories, symbols, and objects.

That is why marketers pay millions to celebrities to take pictures with their products even if the celebrity says in public that he doesn't even use the product. Do you really feel like buying Hanes underwear just because Michael Jordan wears them in a commercial? Maybe not. But if he didn't sell more underwear, the company wouldn't keep paying him.

Music, smells, and symbols are great at creating association. Did you know that the average American child recognizes McDonald's golden arches before he is even 20 months old? It's true. I once had an employee whose son spoke three words: Mama, Didy, and McDon. The funny part is, this kid hardly ate at McDonald's. The family was strict Muslim- they ate only Halal (similar to Kosher).

HOW OTHERS USE THIS

Credit card companies are great at using imagery and association. Studies found that people using credit cards spend more money than if they pay in cash. They also tip better. Not only that, but they spend more even if just the logo of a credit card is displayed.

When a room full of subjects was asked to donate to charity, 87% donated when MasterCard logos appeared in the room. Without the logos, only 33% donated. **Even more amazing is that the charity did not even accept credit cards for the donations!**

Most U.S. presidents have pet dogs. Why? Because the American public has a positive feeling about the owner of a loving, obedient, trusting dog. Many things we take for granted are planted.

HOW WE CAN USE THIS

Have a picture of a cute dog in your office. It will give you something to talk about.

Use a symbol or logo that describes your USP.

A particular title company rep wanted to be known for fast service. So she always wore bright-color sneakers: red, yellow, and pink. They stood out. On her business card and stationary she had the same theme with sneakers and a slogan.

Our company logo is a tree with money falling to the ground. It fits with our name, MoneyTree Mortgage.

Colors are used as symbols. The graphic of a handshake is used by many to convey trust. Two hands cupped together show protection and safety. Gold and currency convey wealth.

How can you make your USP visual? What are some of the symbols that you see other companies use?

Using these psychological factors in your business, will dramatically increase your conversion rates. Be warned: there is a lot of material in this chapter. Every time you read it, you will get more ideas on how to implement the factors to your benefit.

WINNING
NEGOTIATIONS

Real estate is one of the few places (other than car dealer-ships) where negotiation is the rule rather than the exception. It takes a keen understanding of the homebuyer's viewpoint to be good at negotiating.

All elements of the purchase agreement are negotiable, not just the price.

This is a statement that home buyers hear from all sides. Many buyers will take this information to heart and try to shave your fees along with other costs and fees associated with the sale. It's part of the game to them.

What's a mortgage professional to do? While there is no hard and fast rule to apply to every single transaction, there are points to keep in mind that can help you get your fees without reducing them.

NEGOTIATING MYTHS AND REALITIES

We have all been there at some stage—the dreaded negotiation with an awkward client. There are a lot of myths surrounding negotiating which don't help if you are faced with handling such a session. But as with any myth, there is usually a very different reality.

Myth: It can be a daunting ordeal

The majority of people think that negotiating is a dirty and tough task, a necessary evil.

Reality: Not if you plan

As with other things in life, we fear the unknown, especially if we are unprepared. The reality of negotiating is that with adequate preparation comes confidence. Ask yourself the following questions:

- What do you want out of this negotiation?

- What is your lowest, acceptable and best price?

- What are you prepared to 'give away' if necessary?

- What do you know about the client's position in the deal?

Thorough preparation is a great confidence booster. See the negotiation as a presentation and plan your approach and questions before hand.

Myth: Negotiators are born

There is such a fog surrounding negotiation and the skills needed to be good at it that most people think you either have it at birth or you don't.

Reality: Negotiators can be made

Like any skill in business, negotiation skills can be learned and improved as they are put into practice. Negotiation is a structured process and once you understand how it all works the task becomes easier. But as with any new skill you have to practice, practice, practice and this is where most people fail.

Myth: To strike a deal you have to concede on price

The perception is that many negotiations end up with one of the parties (you) always having to concede just to secure the deal.

Reality: There are other items you can concede on

The reality in any negotiation is that price is not always the deciding factor. There is usually something else that the other party wants in addition to, or instead of, a lower price. It could be that they need the service quickly and may be prepared to pay a premium for fast delivery. They may want things changed slightly to meet their specifications. They may like more hand-holding and will pay for that.

In your research and questioning it's up to you to find out what they really want. Dig deep and find it because every part of the deal is negotiable, not just the price. Once you have hit upon it, before conceding on price, throw it into the pot. Remember, this could be something which means very little to you but a lot to them.

Myth: Negotiating is a competition with only one winner
If you have a competitive streak this is how you will see a negotiation—something to win or lose. Non-competitive people who believe this myth automatically lower their defenses and quickly cave in to the "stronger" player.

Reality: There should be two winners
Negotiation is not a competition. The ideal outcome should be win-win, where both sides feel they achieved something out of the whole process—one got a loan with a fair amount of profit and the other got a loan at a rate he wanted.

Win-win outcomes leave the door open for building strong relationships which will lead to more business in the future. Win-lose outcomes mean that one side will be reluctant to deal again. If, by your very nature, you are a competitive person, temper this and accept the reality that the negotiation process has to have two winners, not just you!

Myth: If you walk away, that's it

You are afraid to lose the deal so you decide to go for it anyway, at any price.

Reality: Opportunities often come around again

Accepting a deal through fear is not a position you want to be in. You will always have a nagging doubt that you gave away too much. Be strong enough to say no to a loan if it's not good for you.

Take a look at your view of negotiating. Are you clinging onto old myths about how negotiating should be done? Consider that the reality may be very different.

WHAT YOUR CLIENTS ARE BEING TOLD

There is a large body of knowledge and advice available to home buyers that covers all aspects of the process of buying and financing, including your services and fees. Understanding the advice they are being given will help you received the fees you want.

Here are examples of "tips" that are available to home buyers in various forms. You can find other information by browsing the Internet using a "client's eyes."

Superior knowledge gives you the edge in negotiations.

The National Association of Realtors reports that more than 77 percent of buyers now begin their purchase research on the Internet. Additional buyer research sources include newspaper real estate home sections, newspaper classified ads and local home-buying magazines.

Find out as much as possible about the other party.

Learn as much as possible about the other party to the negotiation while revealing as little as possible about your motivations. In real estate negotiation, if you are a highly motivated buyer or seller, chances are the other party will get the best of you.

Avoid showing your emotions.

Smart negotiators never show their emotional involvement. In other words, no matter how much you want or need to buy a home (or anything), don't telegraph your emotions so the other party can gain the negotiation edge.

He who cares least wins.

If you absolutely must quickly buy or sell a home, you're not in a strong negotiation position. Instead, try to avoid getting into that "must win" situation.

Don't get involved in an involuntary auction.

Professional negotiators often pressure buyers into an immediate purchase decision by saying another party is interested in buying the same property. The best way to combat an involuntary negotiation auction situation, unless you enjoy bidding competition, is to temporarily walk away. If you're told there is another buyer making an offer, but you really want the property, you could write in your purchase offer, "I will exceed any other valid purchase offer obtained on this property within five days by $3,000." This prevents the negotiation auction from getting out of the buyer's control.

Go for a win-win negotiation.

Buyers and sellers, as well as their agents, should aim for a win-win negotiation outcome where both parties get what they want without giving up too much. In other words, both sides feel satisfied with the result.

After the transaction successfully closes, be sure to congratulate the other party and their agent on their skillful negotiation—even if you think you were the most successful negotiator.

CONVINCING THE BUYER TO PAY YOUR PRICE

Many loan officers are afraid to stand by their fee structure because of a mistaken assumption: "If I refuse to negotiate, I'll lose my customer." This is highly unlikely. Still, it is safe to assume that you will be asked to lower your fees fairly often. Here are some fundamental ideas that can help from your "ground of being," your philosophy, about your fee structure and your willingness to negotiate them.

You are entitled to reasonable compensation.

Just as your doctor, your accountant, and your plumber are entitled to a reasonable compensation for their services, you are entitled to a reasonable compensation for your service. What is reasonable? Basically, whatever your buyer believes that your service is worth. The operative principle here is value. No buyer will begrudge you a fee that is reasonable relative to the perceived value of your service.

Don't sell yourself short.

Do you believe that your services are worth the price? If the answer is yes, then you should expect to receive a worthy price. If you lack confidence about your service, buyers will become aware of your doubts. Don't sell yourself short.

Don't apologize.

Once you have established the value of your services, present your fee information with confidence. Never apologize for your price. If you believe your price is correct, just assume that your customers will agree.

Always be willing to walk away.

You must be prepared to say "Next!" or your customers will sense your uncertainty. The willingness to walk away from a transaction comes from having options. It is crucial to have other potential sales in the line-up. When you know that your career doesn't hinge on this one deal, you can exude confidence. And buyers will bow to confidence.

Even if your career does depend on this one deal, do not let it show. Borrowers can sense it when they have the upper hand. Remember, you are the professional.

Make the buyer work for concessions.

If you appear too anxious to negotiate your price or terms downward, the buyer will perceive you as worth less (or maybe even worthless). Don't give in right away. Ask for concessions in return, such as additional business.

Qualify your prospective buyers.

There are occasions where you may be wasting your time negotiating with a customer. If you think a buyer may be out of your range (either below it or above it), ask: "What kind of budget are we looking at?" or "What range are we looking at here?" You may want to let them know that you are not in the same range.

The major obstacle that prevents salespeople from receiving the fee they want is the fear of rejection. One way of dealing with this fear is to lower your price. A better way is to overcome your fear by schooling yourself in assertive negotiation techniques. When you do it right, both you and your customer will feel a sense of satisfaction. Ultimately, your belief in yourself and your service will be your best weapon. Your confidence will be rewarded.

HOW TO JUSTIFY YOUR PRICE

Once you have decided on your fee structure, you need to provide reasonable justification so your buyer will say, "Okay, that makes sense. I can accept that." Here are some approaches to educating clients to understand your fee structure.

Begin with benefits.

"That's my fee for this type of work." Instead of springing an unsubstantiated fee on a client, start every sales process by identifying the client's desired benefits, and then quantify them. It's hard work, but it pays off when you eventually get to a discussion of fees. With a credible estimate of benefits, the client has a powerful context to evaluate whether your fee is a good deal.

Know four reasons why.

To many clients, fees associated with home financing are a black box. Address your part of the equation by being prepared to give clients at least four good answers to the question, "What is your fee based on?"

Beware of ballpark estimates.

Clients may ask for "ballpark" fee estimates (GFE) before all the facts are on the table. The danger with ballpark estimates is that they tend to stick in clients' minds. Tossing out fee estimates before you've grasped the nuances of a particular transaction can put you in a tough position once you've arrived at an actual fee. If your actual fee differs from your ballpark estimate—and it usually does—you have to begin the conversation about fees by explaining all the reasons why your ballpark number missed the mark, not why the fee is appropriate for the job at hand.

Your prospective client will be frustrated if you stonewall the ballpark estimate question, but resist the pressure. Ask for some breathing room to create a fee estimate that's based on fact, not fiction. Create your estimate carefully, but quickly, and you and the client won't end up in a classic "lose-lose" situation.

Negotiate with the client, not with yourself.

When a sale is imminent, it's easy to get swept up in the moment. Your thoughts may drift to the ancillary benefits of serving a new client: selling follow-on work, developing new relationships, securing a reference client, improving visibility and gaining an opportunity to do new work.

As you engage in an internal dialogue about these benefits, the stakes for closing the sale may begin to rise. You might think, "The potential for creating a more profitable practice in the future could ride on landing this deal." This line of reasoning often leads a person to consider reducing fees to make sure the deal isn't lost.

When you're lowering fees based on those expectations, you're negotiating the fee with yourself, instead of with your client. More often than not, you'll leave money on the table when you negotiate with yourself.

Don't price on futures.

Some loan officers reduce fees for the initial deal in the misguided belief that such a gesture will set them up for winning future deals at standard rates. This strategy rarely works.

Most brokers find it nearly impossible to push rates to pre-discount levels simply because a new deal is gearing up. If you want to try for higher fees, prepare for resistance. Once you establish a client's perception of your value, it's going to take more than a new deal to change that perception.

Whatever you do, remember that your objective is to create a satisfied customer. The more you provide satisfaction (i.e., good customer service) throughout the process, the better off you'll be when your client starts hinting about lowering your fees. It's even possible that they won't even ask about lowering the fee because they are so satisfied with your service that they can't bring themselves to pay you less!

WHEN TO NEGOTIATE AND NOT NEGOTIATE YOUR PRICE

You want to leave yourself the option of negotiating a lower price if it is in *your* best interest to do so. The operative principle here is called "saving face." In other words, you will lower your price only if you can save face, i.e., maintain the integrity of your basic fee structure. So you tell your customer, "I accept a lower price only under the following circumstances ..."

What are those circumstances? You might consider offering a discount if you get assurance from the customer that they will come to your for the next (confirmed) deal(s), is already a repeat customer, or has already referred business to you.

If the demand or request is not possible, too demanding, or not reasonable for any reason, you must kill it then and there, or it will come back to haunt you. Do not negotiate if there are unrealistic demands being made at any stage. This is for three reasons.

- It prevents you having to concede substantial ground unnecessarily.

- It avoids raising false hopes, which would make it difficult for us later to satisfy later.

- It stamps your personal authority and professionalism on the situation.

A clear and honest "No, I'm afraid not," with suitable explanation and empathy for the other person's situation is all it takes.

TYPICAL BUYER TACTICS

Here some examples of buyer tactics to open the "lower your fee" conversation. You have likely encountered others.

The Flinch

The buyer says, "Your price is what?!" and they start choking.

Your response:

Silence. They just wanted to see if they could get a reaction out of you. Don't react. It's a test. Be persistent.

The Squeeze

The buyer tells you, "You have to do better!" or "I can get it for less."

Your response:

Sell your unique qualifications. Take the focus off of the price. Get them to agree that yours are the

services they want, and that the price is only a tech-
nicality. If they really want you, they will find a
way to pay for it.

The Sob Story

They cry, "All I have in my budget is..." or "All we can
afford is..."

Your response:

Don't budge. Call their bluff. They may be testing
to see how firm your price is. Ask, "Are there any
other budgets you can draw from?" Their budget
for your service may not be the only one available
to them.

In some cases, you may encounter **The Ultimatum,** with
the client either directly or indirectly saying "Lower your fee,
or I'll take my business elsewhere." If you do end up on the
receiving end of this tactic, one question to ask yourself is how
did you get to this point? Have you been diligent with this
client, and provided them the best service you possibly could?
If so, consider using some of the principles of persuasion to
influence your client to back down from their position. If not,
see what you can do to fix the relationship.

If you have done all you can think of, and the client is
standing firm, you will have to choose whether to lower your

fee or stay put. **Remember that your client has a face to save too, so you may need to come up with a mutually face-beneficial solution: for example, counteroffer a fee somewhere between yours and the one the client proposes.**

1. Don't look at the deal as an either/or choice.

Good negotiating is about compromising where both sides get what they want. Everything is negotiable. The prospect has more that we want than just money. If they want to pay less, come up with alternatives that they could pay you in lieu of a large fee. Can you barter for services? Can the client get you into the country club? Can the client arrange a meeting with his realtor? The possibilities are endless.

2. Know what you can give up—then do so reluctantly.

If you have a feeling a particular client is going to hammer you on every line of the GFE, you need to add items that can be removed. This way, he saves face, you get what you want, and the deal goes through.

Have a list of your minimums. Know what you can and can live without in every loan.

3. Use time on your side, if you can.

Many times, interest rates are going up, or at least they could. Sometimes a buyer needs to close within a certain amount of days and is under the gun. Use the lack of time on your side, by sticking to your guns and justifying it because of the lack of time.

4. Make sure you make the clients feel that you understand their position.

When dealing with a tough client, rapport can help calm things down. Make your clients view you as an ally, not an enemy. Mirror their emotions. Empathize with them. Be an advisor, not a salesman.

5. Keep your emotions in check.

Don't take it personally when a client tells you bluntly that he doesn't think you are worth your fee. Or that you are trying to rip him off. Keep your cool and you have a greater chance of prevailing.

On the flip side, do not hesitate to raise your fees. Stating that you charge 2 points origination is as easy as saying you charge 1 point. Doing it with confidence and in a matter of fact manner will convince the client that this is common in your business, even if it is not, and will not cause them to question it. If you state your fees in an apologetic fashion than you will be questioned even if you are charging only half of one percent origination.

6. Don't believe everything.

In a tough negotiation, you need to realize that things will be said that might not be true. There might not be another company offering a .25% lower rate. But if you call the client a liar, you will still lose the loan. Pride is worth more to most people than money. Plus, we want to get referral and repeat business out of each client.

Kindly restate your position and talk about how because rates have increased, there is no way anyone can offer a lower rate.

7. Be prepared to walk away.

If the client refuses to give, you have the option of canceling the loan. Some loans are just not worth it. If the client is willing to fight tooth and nail from the beginning, he is going to be a tough person to work with through the whole deal.

If you are prepared to walk away, you will not come off as desperate. And that will make the client want to deal with you even more. If you seem desperate, clients will use that against you.

In the end, it is up to you how much to negotiate and where to draw the line. As far as money is concerned, my personal policy is not to lock a loan until I have a filled out application, a check for the appraisal, and one for the credit report. Only then will I proceed. We are not in business to be giving out GFEs to everyone that calls. And there is no way I am paying for a credit report for a lookie-lou.

"I DON'T WANT TO PAY ORIGINATION!"

We have all heard this many times. Either the person doesn't want to pay origination and still wants the best rate or they want us to cut our fees.

When you deal in a small community where the companies know each other the situation can get pretty tense. Like for my church, we have about 10,000 members around Houston. And there are about 10–15 members that are loan officers or have their own company. When someone from church is referred to me, they usually know at least one other loan officer in church. And since many of these guys don't know anything about service, the only thing they know how to do to get a client is reduce the fees. Sometimes they don't even charge origination. They are just happy with the processing fee.

So how do we deal with someone who wants us to cut our fees?

First, you need to differentiate yourself. You need to make them want to do business with you. What do you bring to the table no one else does? Wow them with Amazing Service™ as soon as they call or walk in the door.

This is where your USP comes in. Most of your competition will be competing on price. You need to compete on something else. Make sure your prospects know that price is not the most important issue at stake.

Second, make sure they know why you charge the fees. Having a list of all the things you do works great here. Make a list as long as you can of all the actions your company undertakes during a loan. Use this as a visible tool. It doesn't matter if every company does the same thing—you can be sure they do not educate the customer on what they do for them.

So show them. Title the list: 101 Things (company name) Does for Each Customer. When showing them the list, go over a few of the points. And make sure to tell the prospects that, "With another company, you cannot be sure what you will get. It is easy to promise, hard to deliver. We guarantee to do all these items for you."

Do not let them take this list home to show to the other company. Keep one laminated at your desk and use it whenever you need.

Third, explain to them how Yield Spread Premium works. Show them that either they can pay in fees or by paying a higher rate. Your prospects might already know this. If they don't, inform them that you will get them a lower rate. If they still do not want to pay as much in fees, offer them a higher rate in exchange for all your fees.

Fourth, if they want a higher rate, fine. But make sure they know that fees paid are tax deductible in the year of the purchase. By having a higher rate they will pay much more interest for years to come. If you have amortization software like ProEdge you can show them printouts of how much interest they will be paying extra.

Fifth, here are some of the scripts I have advised my coaching clients to use in this situation.

1. Look them straight in the eye and seriously tell them, "You might get another loan officer desperate enough to lower the fees, but I run a class act, and I don't do business that way."

2. Put the ball in their court by answering with a question, "Why do you feel I need to lower my fees?" This usually causes them to hem and haw since they don't have a legitimate reason except that they want to negotiate.

3. Show them that you are taking all the risk. "Sure, I will lower my fees. In fact I will cut them in half, if you pay upfront in advance."

4. Tell them lower fees are only an option for those that send you referrals or repeat customers. "If you were in our gold customer group, you would qualify for lower fees. But unless you join that group I cannot lower my fees, because it would not be fair to my best customers."

Sixth, if you must absolutely reduce the fees, ask them to give up something as well. Don't agree to less money without getting a concession from them. It could be that they have to introduce you to their realtor, allow you to send a letter of introduction to their sphere of influence, give you three names of people thinking of moving, or whatever you want. Maybe you don't want them calling you more than two times a day. It could be anything. But make sure you get something.

Seventh, have a junk fee that you can throw out. If they want lower fees, and they won't budge, agree to throw out the mortgage broker fee of 1%. Or the application fee, or any other fee you normally do not charge.

If you work mainly on referrals, you will not run into this as much as with cold leads. But you must be ready for it because it will come. Some cultures and people just negotiate everything. That's part of game. Going through these seven steps with your prospects will satisfy their objection most of the time.

SECTION 5

30 Days To Success

Congratulations. You now know more than 95% of loan offi-cers in this country about how to run your business as a business, how to generate enough leads to achieve your goals, and how to use psychology to convert those leads into loans.

This final section brings it all together. The final chapter is an actual 30 day plan that you can follow to Jump Start Your Mortgage Career. The plan covers what we have already discussed and tells you exactly what to do and in what order. It's time to get off your duff and start using some of the things you just learned throughout this book.

This plan has been tested by myself and my coaching clients. We played with it, tried it out, and tweaked it until it was the most effective we could make it. Follow the plan, and you will succeed.

This is where the rubber meets the road. How serious are you in your new career? We will see. This plan is not easy. In fact, it will probably take you a lot longer than the 30 days that it has been designed for.

This plan leaves no room for weekends off. You can take weekends off when you start cashing those commission checks. But first you need to set up your business, design it, pour the foundation, and get the gears churning.

This plan is a crash course in mortgage success. It is eventually up to you to do it or not. But since you have come this far, why not take the final step and put what you have learned into action? Success requires action. And this is your chance to show what you can do.

As you progress, I would love to hear from you. Make sure to drop me an email. Let me know how you are doing or if you have any questions. Remember, my company and I are here for you.

30 DAYS
TO SUCCESS

Listed below is a plan for you to follow. It will probably take you longer than 30 days. But it is laid out for you to achieve quick success. And that is what I want for you. Not gradual and slow, but quick and now.

One point I want to make is that there are no days off. If you work according to this plan, you will work on weekends. From my experience, many new loan officers want to work. They want to move quickly to start having leads and loans coming in. If this does not describe you, then take your weekends off, and continue from where you left off. The days are set so that you follow one after another. They are not meant to allow you to skip around and pick and choose what you want to do.

The plan will work best if you do all the activities as they are described in the order they are laid out in.

Ready? Here we go...

Day 1:

1. Reread Chapters 1, 9, and 10

2. Establish your goals—both personal and professional. Where do you want to be in one year? Five years? Ten years? Only by having proper goals will you ever attain all that you seek. Have your goals in writing and review them at least once per day.

3. Know your numbers. Do not overlook this very important step. Do all the calculations to determine how many leads you need. Have two sets of numbers—one that allows survival, and the other to achieve your goals.

Day 2:

1. Reread Chapter 2.

2. Research the different examples of niches and brainstorm some of your own. What niches are you already a part of? What groups would you fit in with? Once you have some potentials, identify the demographics of the groups. Are they large enough? Do they make enough money? Will you be able to penetrate the group?

3. Choose at least one niche on which you will focus.

Day 3:
1. Reread Chapter 3
2. Create your own USP. It must be something that will make people want to do business with you. How can you separate yourself from the pack?
3. Make sure your USP is on all your marketing materials. This includes business cards, signs, ads, and every piece of literature that leaves your office. Your USP is no good if people do not know about it.

Day 4:
1. Reread Chapter 7
2. Create a personal mission statement. Without a rudder, your boat will go wherever the tide takes it. Your personal values and mission are what will guide your destiny.
3. Create a business mission statement. Your business should mirror your personal values and ethics. A properly formed business mission statement will help you in making hard decisions that will test your value systems.

Day 5:
1. Reread Chapter 4
2. Put together your Sphere of Influence. Create a massive list of as many people as you know.
3. Once identified, collect their contact information.

4. Organize this information so that you can access it quickly, by using either a software program or a simple card system.

Day 6:

1. Reread Chapter 6.
2. Create your own Business Plan.

Day 7:

1. Create a letter to send to your Sphere of Influence. If you are new, let everyone know that you are now in the mortgage business. If you are not so new, apologize for not staying in touch and let them know that you will from now on.
2. Create your daily time schedule and make sure to include time everyday to market. Set aside times each day for marketing. Aim to always do at least one action each day that will result in having more leads.

Day 8:

1. Analyze what other loan officers are doing in terms of marketing. What seems to be working? What doesn't? Are they just copying each other? Does any loan officer or mortgage company stand out from the rest? Look in the yellow pages, weekly shopper newspapers, check out local company websites, etc.
2. Create a list as long as you can of potential prospecting techniques, channels, and mediums you might use to distribute

your message. How will you get your message to your target niche? You should have at least 30–40 different options at your disposal.

Day 9:

1. Create your Marketing Plan.

Day 10:

1. Start mailing out the letters you wrote to your Sphere of Influence. Twenty per day is a good number to start with. Continue until you have them all mailed out.

Day 11:

1. Register your own Internet domain name. You eventually will need a website. Domain names are going fast. Choose one or more that describe you or your niche. Try to get the .com and .net extensions. Keep it easy to remember and spell.

Day 12:

1. Come up with way to stays in contact with your Sphere of Influence **every month.** You need to stay in their conscious mind. The best way to do that is to stay in front of them. You can use monthly mailings, print newsletter, email newsletter, postcards, gifts, etc.

2. Lay out your monthly contacts one year in advance. That way you know and can prepare for what will be sent and when it should be ordered or created by.

Day 13:

1. Make sure you understand the 1003 loan application form and Good Faith Estimate. Fill out several of them as practice until you can fill them out with your eyes closed. These two forms are the ones most likely to trip up new loan officers in the initial interview. It breeds fear in the minds of the prospects when their loan officer cannot answer the most basic questions.

2. Come up with a list of the most commonly asked questions by prospects and their answers. You can either ask your broker, fellow loan officers, or check out the questions answered in the many books on home buying at the bookstore.

Day 14:

1. It has been four days since you started mailing your letters to your Sphere of Influence. It is time to start calling them.
   a. Ask if they got the letter.
   b. Inform then that you will be happy to answer any questions they ever have about real estate and financing.
   c. Ask if they know anyone that could use your services right now.

Day 15:

1. Reread chapters 11 and 12.
2. Choose two methods of prospecting to start with. Make sure they fit within your budget and the results can be tracked. Make sure to track your leads on a daily basis. You should know where every lead came from.

Day 16:

1. Brainstorm ways to follow up with all prospects. Most people who call you will either not need your services right away or will need more convincing before they trust you. A proper follow-up system is crucial to your success.
2. After you have chosen, implement your system. Make sure to include at least three follow-ups for every lead. Marketing studies have shown that close to 80% of all sales occur after the fifth contact.

Day 17:

1. Reread Chapter 16.
2. Choose three or four psychological factors to help you convert leads.
3. Implement the use of those factors into your business.

Day 18:

1. Call up several local and national mortgage companies posing as a prospective borrower. Do they make it easy or hard to deal with them? Do they distinguish themselves from each other? How is their customer service?

2. List all the things that the companies did well, and what they did poorly.

3. Use this knowledge to come up with ways to WOW your prospects. How can you prove to someone that working with you means working with a professional that knows what Amazing Service™ is all about?

Day 19:

1. Design your initial interview. When you first meet with a prospect, what impression will you make? What will you say? A structured interview will make sure you get all your goals of the meeting met and that the meeting stays on course.

   - Come up with the questions you will ask the prospects to generate rapport.
   - Come up with the flow of the meeting—introduction, initial questioning, small talk, answering their questions, pre-qualifying, 1003, etc.

Day 20:

1. Become familiar with the most popular loan programs in your marketplace. Determine if you have enough loan programs to handle most prospects. The more programs you offer, the more leads you can try to convert. In the beginning it will be important to not have to turn away any prospective loans. As your business matures, you can decide to restrict the programs you offer.

2. If you need more lenders, get them.

Day 21:

1. Reread chapter 13.

2. Decide if having a website is something you want to do right now. If your prospects have been asking for it, then perhaps you should have one.

3. If you decide that you need one, you must decide to either get one from a website vendor, or to have it created from scratch. Both sides have their pros and cons. But at this point in your career, having a website designed from scratch will take up a large chunk of your time, time that can be better spent prospecting for business.

Day 22:

1. Analyze your prospecting so far. Have you been tracking your leads? How is your marketing doing? Keep in mind that less than 1% response can be acceptable in many instances. We do not need a home run. We want a dependable source of leads than can get us on base month after month. If your lead source is not producing as much as you would like, consider tweaking it. If it is a total failure, replace it with another method.

Day 23:

1. Reread Chapter 8
2. Come up with ways to automate or outsource your prospecting. As your marketing starts generating leads, you will have to find a way to have those leads handled, either by machine or by someone else. That way you can concentrate on your business.

Day 24:

1. Tape record your initial interview with a live prospect. Listen to it and critique yourself. We often feel that we perform better than we actually do. Recording your conversation gives you unbiased feedback.

Day 25:

1. Devise a way to reward referrals. You must have a way to provide positive feedback to someone when they refer you a loan.

2. Determine how you will thank borrowers after their loan closes. Many loan officers provide a thank you gift. I recommend throwing them a house warming party at their house and letting them invite their friends and family. This way you can be introduced to everyone and get a silent testimonial as well. They key is to be remembered.

Day 26:

1. By now, you should have a good idea of how many leads your prospecting is churning out. If you can handle it, consider adding a third method of prospecting for even more leads.

Day 27:

1. Spend time with a processor in the office. Learn the procedures of processing. By taking time to do this you can answer more of your prospects questions right away instead of having to ask the processor. You can also discover ways to help your loans get through processing more quickly by learning some of the tricks of the trade.

Day 28:

1. Take a successful loan officer out to lunch or go with a wholesale lender's representative. Learn from others in the business. You can also learn a lot from a title company representative or a closing attorney. Ask lots of questions. Build a friendship.

Day 29:

1. Review and log your numbers for the month. Analyze them to see what your efforts have accomoplished. You have been at this for almost a month. How are you doing? A monthly review session can keep you on track. Do this every month. Make adjustments where necessary. Adjust your marketing plan if needed. And remember to keep striving toward your goals. Do not let your destination out of your sight.

Day 30:

1. Consider taking the Jump Start Your Mortgage Career Online E-Class for a greater edge in this business. There is no way to cover all you need to know in one book. But in the course, I have no limitations. If anything, you will say the course has too much information. Once you get a handle on all this material, the next logical step would be to take the e-class. But make sure you know and understand everything presented here first.

Congratulations. You made it. You have learned and done a lot in a short amount of time. What you just did takes most loan officers over a decade to learn and figure out. Many never do. But the question is now—what will you do? Will you use this information and the techniques to continue to improve, or will you slide back to the comfort zone you were in when you started this program?

Your success depends on the actions you take. I am here rooting for you. I will be behind you all the way. Between the two of us, there is nothing that can stop us. Let's make your career and your life spectacular!

INDEX

Pricing structure, niche
marketing and, 41
Pride, goal setting and, 6
Principles, core, 146, 147
Prioritization
business plans and, 134
goal management and,
17, 21–22
marketing contacts
and, 209
mission statements
and, 140, 142
time management
and, 99–100
Privacy concerns, 243
Procrastination, 110–115,
119, 131, 163
Proctor, Craig, 109
Product planning, 122
Professional associations,
222–223
Profit, new business and,
167–168
Profit and loss statements,
127
Property types, niche
marketing and, 36
Prospects. *see also* Lead
generation
30 days to success plan
and, 371, 374–375
conversion rates and. *see*
Conversion rates
defined, 178
getting business from,
301–303
influence over. *see*
Influence
niche marketing and,
31–32
unique selling
proposition and, 66–70
Psychology, 303. *see also*
Influence
The Psychology of Influence,
307

Public appearances, 166
Public servants, niche
marketing and, 52
Publicity, 208

R
Rainmaker theory, 165–166
Rapport, 315
Rates, xiv, xvi, 235, 288,
290–292
Reading, 97, 98–99, 101–102,
366–377
Real estate agents
approaching, 269–272
common practices to earn
business, 273–276
concerns of, 258
desires of, 268–272
lead generation and, 191
marketing and, 227
Marketing to Real Estate
Agents Toolkit, 264, 278,
279–282
mentality of, 257
pitfalls and, 266–267
strategies, advanced,
277–279
three pillars and, 196–197
training of, 258
types of, 276
working with, 259–265,
268
Real Estate Agents Toolkit,
198
Real estate investment
groups, 226
Real Estate Settlement
Procedures Act (RESPA),
268
Reciprocity, law of, 306–310
Reeves, Rosser, 66
Referrals
being referable and,
292–293
benefits of, 288–292

closing rates and,
287–288
conversion rates and,
187–188
defined, 178, 283
generation of, 293–296
importance of, 283–287
involvement, law of
and, 333
niche marketing and, 197
real estate agents and,
259–260, 275
rejection and, 218
rewards for, 375
Total Client Value (TCV)
and, 83, 84–85
tracking, 172, 176
Referrals on Demand
System, 198
ReferralsOnDemand.com,
184
Rejection, 217–218, 348
Relationships, existing,
208–210
Religious groups, niche
marketing and, 53
Relocation, niche marketing
and, 54
Remax, 109
Repetition, 334
Resentment, procrastination
and, 111
Resources
AnyBrowser.com, 242
BNI.com, 216
Builder.com, 242
business plans, 137
classes, xvii
Elance.com, 240
Inventory.Overature.com
/d/SearchInventory/
Suggestion, 239
making plans and, 15
MortgageBrokerTraining.
com, 240

WARNING: 82% OF LOAN OFFICERS DO NOT PRODUCE ENOUGH LOANS TO LAST MORE THAN 2 YEARS IN THE MORTGAGE BUSINESS.

… what 1 simple step can you take to make sure this doesn't happen to you?

The Jump Start Your Mortgage Career E-Class is your next step to mortgage success.

Here is a taste of some of the things you will learn in the online course:

- **A way to double your closings without any extra leads.**

- **How to set up your business so that if you took a one month vacation you would still have a thriving business when you got back.**

- **7 ways to get realtors to give you ALL their business.**

- **The 7 steps I use when someone tells me to lower my fees.**

- **How to get all the FREE advertising you want.**

- **How "the halo effect" can get you loads of qualified prospects seeking you out.**

- **The one technique that brings in more referrals than all others combined.**

- How to generate customers with zero acquisition cost.

- How NOT to get business from realtors. Why most loan officers waste their time and money and never get any business from realtors.

- 69 ways to market to borrowers that work.

- Don't just master your business career, but learn to master the 5 other areas of your life for true peace of mind.

- Over 3 dozen marketing ideas that cost less than $100 each to implement and work like gangbusters!

- When to flaunt your personality in your business and when not to—Do this properly and customers will flock to you. Do it wrong, and you will offend them.

- How "souvenirs" can make you hundreds of thousands in commissions.

- Why, according to *Sales And Marketing* magazine, 80% of all people who inquire about a product buy within one year—but not from the company that made the original contact, and how to make sure this never happens to you.

- Why you should never market to "anyone who wants a mortgage".

- The #1 most important business secret in the mortgage biz. Ignore this and you are condemning yourself to a life of gut wrenching prospecting forever.

- And many more.

22 lessons taught by your own personal instructor. It doesn't matter if today is your first day in the mortgage business or if this is your 35th year. If you could use more business, this course is for you.

Top producers all have one thing in common: They know how to market themselves. That is what this course will teach you.

We guarantee that this course will work for you or your money back. And we have made it affordable for all loan officers. In fact, you should get at least 3–4 loans from what you learned in the course even before you finish the course!

Give yourself a head start. Learn from the mistakes and successes of others. Jump Start Your Mortgage Career Today!

Learn more about the class and how to enroll at
www.JumpStartYourMortgageCareer.com

"THE AMAZING SECRETS OF BUILDING A MULTI-MILLION DOLLAR MORTGAGE BUSINESS FROM SCRATCH."

You are sitting at your desk, day dreaming about your upcoming trip to Vegas this weekend, when an associate comes over to talk to you. "Boy, I just hate rate shoppers! Arrrrr! Just lost another loan because somebody quoted a quarter percent less then I did. I was counting on that loan to pay my rent this month," he blurts. Before you can answer, your phone rings. The voice on the line says, "Hi, my name is Jim Smith. I am about to put an offer in to buy a house. I work with Loren Alder; she said she would kill me if I didn't get my loan from you. How soon should we meet to get started?"

Imagine if there was a group of people, say 300 of them. And these 300 people lived normal lives. They did everything the way everybody else does them: work at a normal job, live in an average house, have kids that go to school. Just normal people.

Except, that whenever these people need a mortgage they have to get it from you.

They have no choice in the matter. *As soon as they think of the word mortgage, their brains cause a chemical reaction so that the only person they can think about is you.* Would that help your business? I should say so. If we look at the averages, 10% of these people are going to move every year. That's 30 loans a year coming to you guaranteed. This is the power of *Referrals on Demand.*

Here are even more benefits of the system:

- **Have a steady stream of loans each and every month from your personal sales force.**

- **Instead of being dependent upon advertising for business, you will have realtors, financial planners, and other business owners dependent upon you for referrals.**

- **You will be in control of your business and life by having so many leads and loans, you only have to work with the people who want to work with you.**

- **You do not need to spend money on consumer marketing because you will be able to have leads come to you FREE of charge.**

- **There is nothing for you to write, create, or spend time or money developing. Everything you need is included.**

- **You eliminate the need to compete with other lenders because borrowers will be sent to you already pre-sold on the idea of working with you.**

- You do not have to change or stop doing anything you already do, just add this to it.

You want:

- More loans with less hassle

- Less haggling with customers over fees

- Larger commissions per loan

- Customer Loyalty

- More Time Off Without A Drop in Income

- Referrals generated automatically

- And you want to know if this system can deliver the goods!

Well, guess what? It can and does!

In fact, you will learn how one loan officer using the system, generated 17 loans from one family within 3 months, using only the most basic techniques in the system!

For more info, visit:

ReferralsOnDemand.com

"HOW TO GET AN ENTHUSIASTIC "YES!" FROM REAL ESTATE AGENTS AND BROKERS, EVERY TIME YOU ASK FOR BUSINESS."

Working with just one average realtor can put over $40,000 in your pocket year after year!

Read on to learn how you can get DOZENS of them
to call you,
without cold calling,
without rejection,
without donuts
and without rate sheets.

A realtor called me the other day, and you won't believe what he said,

"Mr. Kamadia, another agent in my office works with you, and she told me this morning how she no longer has to spend any time following up on her leads. She also said how her business has increased as a direct result of working with you. I did over 4 million in sales last year and I would love to meet with you and discuss how we can work together."

He would never have called me if it wasn't for my simple, easy to use, almost-no-work-involved marketing system. My system gets dozens of realtors to call me wanting me to help them increase their business. And because I help them make more money, they give me all their loans and leads. You can easily do the same thing I do.

My new system of getting realtor business has been so successful, I had to hire another assistant!

I call my system, **The Marketing To Agents Toolkit**. It's called a Toolkit because it has everything you need to attract, convert, and get business from realtors. The whole idea that makes the Toolkit so successful is simple. By giving realtors what they want, they give me what I want. Sit up straight and pay attention now because here's the key: I offer realtors something they want—they call me to get it. And when I give them what I promised, I show them something else; something that they cannot live without—and which they can only have, IF they work with me.

When they see what I have to offer, their eyes light up like ten year-olds in a toy store, because they know it could easily double or triple their income in a few months.

Using this system you can easily work
with 10, 20, 30 or more realtors.
If you have ever been rejected by a realtor,
you need to keep reading!

Look how easy it is to use the Toolkit. (NO DONUTS OR RATE SHEETS)

Step 1. Use my ads or letters to offer realtors an information filled "package" that will show them "How to Double Their Income in 90 Days".

Step 2. Once they call you to get this information (no cold-calling), you use the scripts provided to arrange a meeting with the realtor in which you give them the "package."

Step 3. In the meeting you use the other set of scripts included to explain to them the benefits of your "Client Follow-Up System."

For the complete details visit:
MarketingToAgents.com

National Mortgage Trainer Reveals His Secret Weapon To Make Any New Loan Officer More Knowledgeable Than A 10-Year Pro, In 6 days Or Less.
Being a loan officer or mortgage broker without proper mortgage training is like fighting a bear with both hands tied behind your back

To Be A Successful Mortgage Originator There Are 3 Things You Must Know
Item 1: Know the laws and guidelines involved in mortgage originating.
Item 2: Know how to take an application, qualify and place a loan.
Item 3: Know how to get the loan closed.

Residential Mortgage Loan Origination Made Easy
has been written to make sure you know all three.
Item 1. Chapters 5–8 of the manual cover all the laws impacting your mortgage originations, as well as all FNMA loan guidelines.
Item 2. Chapters 9–13 teach you exactly what to do and what to say to customers from an initial meeting through pre-qualification and through application. This includes a line-by-line explanation of both the Good Faith Estimate and the 1003 Loan Application.
Item 3: Chapters 14–17 help you understand what else is involved to close the loan. From locking the loan, to ordering the appraisal, to sending out verifications, to how long it should all take. Everything is covered.

- **How to get your loans approved by FNMA.**

- **Do a full-fledged pre-qualification in less than 5 minutes.**

- Fill out a Good Faith Estimate (GFE) with your eyes closed.

- Complete an entire 1003 application and understand it thoroughly—this includes exercises.

- Complete all FNMA requirements for the property and the borrower.

- Use the tools you need to succeed in this business.

- Understand and interpret rate sheets.

- Obey all laws involved to keep you out of jail.

- Understand B, C, and D markets.

- A review of the widest used mortgage products available today.

- Know the most frequently asked questions by borrowers and their answers.

- Learn how to lock a loan.

- Read a credit report.

- And a lot more.

Check out *www.MortgageBrokerTraining.com* for more info.

AFTER I GIVE YOU MY MOST PRIZED, PERSONALLY TESTED STRATEGIES FOR MAKING TRULY MASSIVE INCOME, IT'LL TAKE KRYPTONITE TO STOP YOU FROM OUT-EARNING EVERYBODY YOU KNOW—

In Fact, You May Want To Keep How Much Money You Make A Secret!

The Millionaire Loan Officer Newsletter is written by someone who is and has been in almost every facet of the industry. The editor is Ameen Kamadia, President of Kamrock Publishing, mortgage consultant, coach and author of this particular book. He is personally responsible for the marketing that has generated hundreds of millions in loan origination revenue.

He started from scratch in almost all his endeavors. He has paid his dues as a credit bureau manager, a real estate agent, a new mortgage broker, an internet marketing newbie, a real estate investor, and a direct marketing student of the masters. He started with little and made his way to the top.

Ameen can show you what works and what does not. Too many mortgage "gurus" keep spouting gimmicks to make themselves rich by selling their stuff. Doing what everyone else does will assure that you will never get ahead of the pack.

Don't do what others have already failed at. Make it easier upon yourself by doing only what has proven to work time and time again. And that is what you will learn in The Millionaire Loan Officer Newsletter.

The Name Is No Accident

Becoming a millionaire is not as hard as some make it out to be. And it is a lot easier if you have a millionaire mentor to show you the way. Each issue of *The Millionaire Loan Officer Newsletter* is chock full of tips, techniques, and strategies that will boost your income tremendously. Page after page of the newsletter is filled with information you can only get from someone who has been there before and is in the trenches everyday.

Every strategy promoted by Ameen has been tested in his own mortgage business. If it works, and only if it works, will he tell readers to do the same thing. Add in the strategies shared with Ameen by his coaching clients, and you have the best mortgage marketing minds sharing what is making them rich beyond their wildest dreams. All this can be yours with a subscription to *The Millionaire Loan Officer Newsletter*. Most of the information that appears in the newsletter is available nowhere else. And it is available to you for just pennies a day.

For more info, visit:
MortgageBrokerTraining.com